Preface

Sometimes things in life come way out of left field and shake you to the core. I had no idea how different events in my life all connected together until I was able to really come into living my own soul purpose. That purpose really came out of nowhere for me. If you would have told me 10 years ago that I would be doing energy healing and would become a voice for children diagnosed with autism, I would have looked at you like you had three heads! Yet, that is what happened. In my private practice, Epiphany Healing Arts, I work with families all over the world, helping to bring deeper understanding of their thoughts, feelings and emotions to the parent's awareness. In this work, many beautiful lessons and miracles have come. As I like to say, "Epiphanies can happen every day." It all started because I learned to listen to my intuition.

CW01499992

Acknowledgements

Thank you for your support, love, inspiration, master teaching and mentoring to:

Troy, Jenna, Michael, Shirley, Don, Steve, James, Alex, Jordan, Jack, Nathalie, Kim, Jennifer, Meg and Uwe.

Thank you to my beautiful animal friends: Pudge, Mac and Cookie who are a huge part of the healing work, inspiration and my guideposts in helping me stay centered every day.

Much gratitude to the beautiful sacred space of Angel Valley, Sedona where I wrote the majority of this book in peace and serenity, inspired by the light and love infusing through the land.

Love to the Thinking Moms' Revolution and their belief in me and in this work.

Thank you to Laura Hirsch for her editing prowess.

Lastly, unending gratitude to my spiritual support team who pushed me out into the world, feeling naked and exposed, the words of my heart bared for all to read, helping me realize that I can do much more than my mind thinks I can.

Vibrational Healing for Autism

(AKA Awesome Kids)

Tami Duncan

Table of Contents

Chapter 1:
A Family Awakening

I never knew what intuition was. I had heard about people having a sixth sense. My mom used to say that she and my grandmother had a keen ability to just know, to just sense when something bad was going to happen. She said it felt like a pit in the bottom of her stomach and then a feeling of dread. I had never felt that before, at least not that I could recall.

As a teenager growing up in Southern California, I just kind of did my thing. I always felt a little left out, and didn't really want to make an effort to join into conversations or make friends with the popular crowd. One good solid friend was good enough for me. It was everything. My best friend Trisha and I met in PE dance class our sophomore year. She was in the back, I was in the front, and somehow we inched our way next to each other without saying a word. Soon we were dance buddies, always dancing side by side every day. That one period class turned into lunch, then hanging out after school, talking about boys for hours and hours. Best friends for life with not much in common except a gentle harmony of personalities that just kind of "got" each other.

Trisha's mom was sick with cancer and early on in our friendship she passed away. As a sixteen-year-old, you really don't know what to do or say. But I felt this Mama Bear protectiveness come over me at school if anyone gave her a hard time. I remember staying after class in

Government to tell off the teacher because he had yelled at Trisha in class. I said very loudly with as much teenage angst as I could muster, matched with the squinty-eyed dirty look I had mastered at that age "HER MOM JUST DIED!" I stomped out as he looked down in shame and apologized.

After that, I knew that I loved her and that our friendship would always be. Who knew that a family tragedy of my own was coming? My brother Steve was 18 at the time, and had just graduated from high school. He was working in the fishing/hunting store and was doing a lot of archery target practice for fun. He was really good at it. Steve was like me in some ways. It wasn't easy for him to make friends, but when he did, they were lifelong.

It was the night of my junior prom. I was dressed to the nines, and my date was over so we could take the standard family prom pictures. My brother watched from the upstairs balcony, looking down in his red plaid flannel shirt. He said, "You look nice." I did a total double take. The look like, "Huh, did you just say something nice to me, what's wrong with you?" This is the look, the vision, that I can see as clear as day nearly 30 years later.

As I danced at prom, the night was just bleh. I looked at my date and thought, "Why?" A feeling came into my heart and I thought to myself, "I should just kill myself." It stayed for a moment until I pushed it aside.

That night, I collapsed into bed with my makeup on. My sleep was disrupted. I heard noises and ringing, saw flashes of light and I was half-asleep and half-awake for what seemed like hours. Suddenly, I heard my mom gently open my door and clear as day in my mind I heard, "My God, he killed himself." As my mom explained what I already knew, I just nodded because I did already know. Every word she said, I knew. How? I don't know. But I did.

Looking back, of course he had obvious signs of depression, but there wasn't a lot of awareness then so we didn't really put it all together. His girlfriend had rejected him for the last time that night and he could no longer take it. A gun to the back of the mouth was his choice. As I look back, I actually could never envision my brother living a long life. I must have always known in some way.

I walked around school numb for days. Many people knew my brother, and either ignored me or embraced me. Even people I didn't really get along with were sending me their love and understanding. I can't say that I accepted it well. I really just felt alone.

Something like that changes you. You begin to look at life differently. I see people fighting with their brother or sister and think, "If ONLY you didn't have them anymore, would you regret the bickering?" I would love for Steve to be back in our physical world. But now I understand that this is not his purpose. Here on Earth is not where he thrives. His purpose is far greater, far grander and exciting than what we do here on Earth. It took a family awakening for me to see, for me to know and to understand the greater purpose of one's experience and the many ways in which we connect and are loved by them.

I never really thought about how I knew he had died even before being told. I just accepted it. One night, I dreamed that Steve and I were sitting on the stairs together as we had many times before, talking. He said, "I'm ok Tami, I'm ok." I felt it was true, I knew. I felt peace in me when I woke up. I hadn't made it up in a dream story. He visited me in spirit and I got it, I received the message loud and clear. It would be several years until I knowingly connected with him again.

College, life, boyfriends, engagements, broken engagements, and finally marriage all sandwiched in my 20's. It wasn't until my beautiful boy Michael was born that things got interesting. My brother was Steven Michael, and his father's name is also Michael, so his name has deep meaning to our families. As he lay in his crib, his blue eyes staring at me, I felt him deeply connect with my soul. A soul recognition to say, "I'm here, we're here together finally and I love you." The message imprinted in my heart for all time. He was less than two months old, and life became about Michael and me from that point on.

One day, I was driving on the freeway with Michael. He was only two years old and began pointing out the window yelling, "It's Jesus! It's Jesus! He's on the side of the road." I saw nothing, but told him I believed him. I did, but I don't know why.

Another time, we brought home a new puppy, a cute little silver schnauzer. I had told Michael many stories about my schnauzer named Pepper growing up. This dog was so special to me that I had wondered if I would ever get married. I'm sure if I could have married the dog I would have! I always told Michael my Pepper stories. When we showed him the new puppy he said, "Mommy, it's Pepper! He came home from heaven!" I said, "No sweetie, this is a new dog, a different dog." He was adamant. "No, THIS IS PEPPER!" I didn't believe him, but we named him Pepper Number 2 anyways. I would later come to find that he was in fact 100% correct. The spirit in this schnauzer body was in fact the same spirit in my Pepper's body. Now that story is for another book.

One day, my mom mentioned that a friend from work was concerned about his mom. She had cancer and was given just days to live. Michael said, "I want to pray for her." He was about five at the time and he said a beautiful prayer. She was released from hospice the next day and lived for another year. I knew it was the power of Michael's prayer that he chose to do from his own sweet heart, without parent or grandparent prodding, his choice. This made me really think, did Michael have some special powers or some direct path to God?

A few years later, a friend brought her son diagnosed with autism over to the house. He was sitting on my couch and had difficulty in moving or holding his body up. Michael went and sat by him, looked at him and held one hand about five inches from the top of his head, closed his eyes and prayed for the boy. I had never seen him do anything like this. It looked like he was sending healing energy to him. As if he had the hand of Jesus held over this boy's head. The boy sat up straight, lifted his head and looked at Michael, and laid back down. He knew something special had happened. Later that day, Michael saw his Naturopath who was amazed and said that his whole body was in a healing state. That had never happened before and then it popped in my mind. When Michael prays or heals, he heals himself.

The evidence was adding up here. I couldn't deny that Michael had some kind of beautiful spiritual connection. He had his own autism diagnosis that we were wrapped in, but that would eventually fade away as he came to know and understand his healing power.

I sought out people to help me. What was going on? Michael would report spiritual beings in his room at night. Some visions were very beautiful and loving and some scary and menacing. I didn't know what to do. I never told him he was seeing things or imagining it. I couldn't, because I was seeing things too, it just took me longer to understand what it was. If I told him he was "hallucinating," then I had to be "hallucinating" too. I wasn't buying it. I much preferred to believe that Michael had some special psychic gifts and maybe I had a smidgen of what he did as well.

I watched as he prayed with his Naturopath to cleanse the energy in the home. They talked to Archangel Michael, asked for protection for all of us. I was sitting on the couch going, "What the hell is happening here?" I couldn't deny the feeling of peace and love emanating from Michael after their sessions. It was real.

I did as every autism momma does, we research. We get online and we Google till we've looked at every search term we can think of and then look at other ones. Words like schizophrenia came up and I raised my middle finger at those and moved on to what felt right, what I knew to be true. Michael was energetically sensitive. I was energetically sensitive.

One night, I had a dream. My friend's little boy came to me in the dream. He was talking to me. I realized something though...in life this boy is considered "non-verbal." How could he talk to me? I said, "Hey, you don't talk in real life." He said, "Oh Tami, I need you to help my mom." I would know later that it wasn't just about his mom, but all moms. He was giving me an introduction to part of my soul's purpose which is to help parents to connect deeply to their children, to hear the unheard, to see the unseen, and to love at the deepest heart level one could ever know.

The Naturopath said that he had sent me this message through telepathy. Wasn't telepathy something like the "Twilight Zone?" She had heard of an energy healer that could do this, she could talk to children who have not developed their speech yet. We called Meg Lupin right away and got in for an appointment. Something was to happen on that day that I will never forget.

As we walked into her home, Michael immediately made himself at home in her office. He looked at her walls, with children's drawings and said, "I remember that place I've been there." He saw a stool and immediately knelt down on it and began to pray. He said, "I remember doing this in Africa." He then told Meg how he knew her in past lives. This went on for an hour. She explained to me how Michael was easily able to connect with his past lives and pull up memories. She talked about his spiritual gifts of clairvoyance and his ability to tell others what their past lives were. This was without thinking, without analyzing. He would do it quick and so matter of a fact that you would think he made it up until you felt the chills run up and down your spine in a full fledge alignment with what he said and a knowing that it was true. I sat there with my jaw on the floor!

Then Weston came. Weston Schmier was 16 at the time and known for his telepathic conversations with Meg Lupin. As his mother, Marilu Schmier, the author of *Waiting for Weston*, talked to me and answered questions about telepathy, Weston just stared at me. At one point I felt a burning in my stomach, he looked at me and I knew he was healing me. As his mom chatted on I thought to myself, "I want to see if I can hear Weston." Since I'm not the chatty type, I began to zone her out and thought really loud in my mind, "Weston, if you can hear me, I can't hear you because your mom is talking too much." All of a sudden Weston began laughing so loud. I thought to myself, "Oh my God he heard me!" Meg told me that yes, in fact Weston had heard me. I had my first "telapthic-ish" experience!

I was completely mesmerized by the concept of telepathy. Was this something I could really do? I made many appointments with Meg, asking her a million and one questions about it. Meg was a Reiki Master. I figured that since she was a Reiki Master and telepathic then if I became a Reiki Master maybe I could be telepathic too.

As I went to my first Reiki class I had a million questions. I wondered if Reiki was always beautiful loving energy or if you could make a mistake and something dark would come in. I learned about how powerful our intentions are and how we can create our own experiences. But the most profound thing that happened that day was during one of the meditations. We were guided to close our eyes and the goal was to go on a meditative journey to meet our spirit guides and our Reiki guides in the spirit world. I had a beautiful experience where I met a guide named Joseph and a Reiki Guide named Angela. These visions popped into my head out of nowhere and they felt very real.

But that wasn't even the good part. One of the ladies in our class named Cindy stated that she couldn't do the meditation. We were all thinking, "Wow, maybe she couldn't relax or something." She said, "No, I am psychic and this spirit kept bothering me." We all sat in focused attention to listen to her story. She talked about a vision of a young man with a scraggly beard, a blue monster truck and trees. She then said, "Who does this guy belong to?" Here's what raced through my mind, "Holy shit, it's my brother!" I meekly raised my hand and she delivered me a message. She said, "He says he is very excited that you are here taking this class and working on your spiritual path. He is very proud of you."

If I could tell you I was completely blown away that would be an understatement. I was a cross between totally freaked out and completely blissful and raging with excitement. I had just experienced, up to that point in my life, the coolest thing ever!

I was hooked. Steve would make his presence known many more times to virtual strangers and deliver messages to me about my path. One time he told a psychic to tell me to pay attention in his class because what he was teaching was important. That night I said, "Steve if you can hear me, play that song we used to listen to on the way to school." I spun the radio dial and within five minutes the song "Walk this Way" by Aerosmith and Run DMC came blasting on the radio. That was it! There was no denying. This…..was…..real!

My world just continued to go along this same path. Major awakenings, learnings and epiphanies were coming my way left and right. The first little boy I worked on who was diagnosed with autism spoke to me telepathically. He heard me and I heard him. Each child I worked on from that point on, I heard, I understood, I knew what they wanted to say. I became the messenger to bring connection to their parents. It is my purpose and my love.

I was remarried to a magnificent guy named Troy during all of this who was and is so supportive. I even tell him of my wacky visions, crazy sounding experiences and he doesn't let on if he thinks I am weird or not. I am so blessed he is in my life to ground me. My daughter Jenna is also a big piece of the puzzle here as she has taught me the amazing lesson of managing one's own energy. She has shown me a mirror of my worst self and my best self many times, and boy is there a lot to learn from that.

On this journey, my learning never stops. Having a certificate of Reiki Master is awesome. But with each and every client session, I am shown new things, new ways of working with energy, and healing issues, and I am forever grateful. These methods come directly from Spirit, from my guides and angels, and if it weren't for my journey up to this point I wouldn't be able to receive this guidance and this blessing.

Then there was Michael. As my gifts flourished so did he. As I realized the power of my words, intentions and how energy worked, he responded. He stepped into his own. He was born a healer and his journey allowed me to awaken my own gifts. A double blessing so it was.

Chapter 2:
Autism and the Spiritual Connection

As our life flows through twists and turns to carry us into the unknown, along the way we shed beliefs that we have been carrying. These beliefs serve as a heavy load and begin to burden us. However, in order to lighten that load we must be open to newness, to new ideas, thoughts and perceptions that we may have never had.

When one speaks of autism and the spiritual connection it can throw us off. Many were raised in religious belief systems that may not allow for this possibility. I ask that you open your heart to the words I share on this topic as the intent is to sprinkle just a little seed in the soil of your mind. If it resonates with you, then allow it to grow and join me in exploring the beauty of the spiritual perception.

My first encounter was with my son Michael. This was described in the earlier chapter, the story of him seeing Jesus and praying for people with astonishing results. I truly did wonder if he had a direct connection to God. But I really wouldn't understand this until I connected with more children than just my son. As I began my energy healing practice, I had just that opportunity. I would speak telepathically to the children and use Reiki and other energy healing to balance their body, mind, emotions and soul level. In that connection is where I learned and still learn the most.

On the outside, a child diagnosed with autism could look agitated, pacing, flicking his hands, repeating phrases over and over. One could assume that child was unintelligent. One could assume he didn't understand what was going on around him. One could assume he didn't pay attention to our conversations or our thoughts. One would be an ass.

Most mothers know that their child is "in there." We may forget and talk around them but when it's quiet at night, the lights are off and all is peaceful, she KNOWS. For me, speaking telepathically and having a heightened sense of empathy and feeling are great tools to understand this more. With every new child I meet, I immediately get a strong sense or feeling of who they are, at their soul level. My soul recognizes their soul as one who I have known before. Information begins to pour in so I may understand them better and translate that to their parents so they can understand too.

I met a boy named Jack a few years ago. When I connected to his energy to do our session for the first time, I had the unmistakable feeling that I was in the presence of an angel....or pretty darn close. His energy field was so pure, so filled with light and he emanated from every cell, every molecule, every part of his aura, pure unconditional love. When you feel this, your mind cannot talk you out of it. It is real.

Kids like Jack are also surrounded by angels and ascended masters, and have knowledge of how to balance their own energy. They don't always choose to, but they do.

When I speak to Jack, he doesn't sound like a five-year-old boy, he sounds like a wise soul with the knowledge and understanding of the ages.

Here's the thing. The mother knows. At a deep place in her, she knows that what I experience with her child is real, it's true. Why? Because she feels it too. She cannot see it during the everyday commotion of life, but deep in her heart she knows her child is special, and emits such incredible love that even she cannot deny. Confirmation of her intuition is all I provide.

Maybe you're thinking, well that's one kid. What about the rest? What about the kids that aren't all angelic and sweet? What about the ones that are violent, aggressive and seem so miserable in their lives? Those kids….those kids seem to be the most highly evolved. The most ascended. Those kids are the ones who look tortured on the outside but on a soul level have made a great sacrifice. Their behavior has purpose, their suffering has meaning. They have made the biggest sacrifice of themselves, their comfort, and their sanity, for what? For all for us.

Soul Purpose

Every soul has a soul purpose. It is predestined before birth. We choose the experiences we would like to have in this time on Earth, although we don't know how it will happen, it will. Many of us have asked for intense learning in this life. Possibly, we need to learn how to take care of our physical bodies with care. Or we would like to learn empathy and compassion for others. Perhaps we would like to expand our spiritual gifts, or finally live by using our intuition. So then to meet our goals, we are given experiences to allow us to learn those lessons. Every life struggle has a lesson, you can learn it or not. But if it is part of your soul purpose and you don't learn that lesson, it will come again, but this time bigger and bolder, and that isn't always comfortable.

As we ask for these lessons in spirit before coming into this body we also have helpers. We are part of a soul group. This is a group of souls that incarnate together for a certain purpose. We make agreements to help each other with our soul purpose. The bigger the experience, the closer our soul is to the other souls involved. Some mothers will secretly tell me that they feel so connected to their son that they feel like their soul mate. I believe them because their souls have so much love connected to them that they would do ANYTHING to help each other. This is where the child diagnosed with autism comes in. He has signed up to help facilitate the lessons that YOU asked for before birth.

Think about some of the lessons you have learned from this autism journey. Have you learned to do your research, how to eat healthy, how to be strong, how to speak your truth? What about the importance of clean water, air and soil? I could go on and on. I know personally I have learned so much on this journey. Each child I talk to is my teacher and my student as our souls work together to align with our soul purpose.

Take a moment and jot down 10 things you have learned about life because of your experience with your child. Now keep this list because it's not to show you how awesome autism is. It's to remind you how rich your journey is and how something that seems so stressful can also include absolutely amazing, beautiful experiences and lessons which is why you came here in this body, in this family, with this kid.

Another point is that the soul purpose shifts as work is complete. So don't think that it will be like this forever. Once we learn the major lessons in which we have asked the child to provide, they can shift into a new purpose and that could be a place of recovery where they can begin living their life in a more comfortable way.

Here's a question you may be wondering. If my child wasn't born with autism how could this be their soul purpose? It's a very good question. The answer is that we are given opportunities in our lives to do our job better. Your child may have chosen that at some time in their life they would have a disability, as they would be able to teach better through that body. Is this why we see some unvaccinated, organically fed, breastfed healthy babies develop autism? Possibly so. Each child, each journey and each purpose is unique, so there isn't a plain answer. But I do know that we are given these opportunities in a divine timing strategy and we can allow it or we can fight it. Even some wise ones take time to come around and understand their brilliance. Those that get it quicker, get through it quicker...the kids and the parents.

Their Special Gifts

Not only do the children sacrifice a great deal in order to help us in this life, they also bring special gifts. Many parents have noticed their children exhibit some seemingly odd behavior. Things like…

- Speaking to a person that isn't there.
- Saying they have spoken to relatives that have passed.
- Knowing your thoughts.
- Saying things like, "My other mom used to…."
- Looking in the corner of the room as if something is there.
- Wanting to look at pictures of angels, Jesus or religious figures.
- Seeing colors around people
- Becoming interested in odd topics like World War I or II, Nazi Germany and saying they have memories of those times.
- Putting their hands on someone looking like they are "healing" something.
- Know complex information that they have not been exposed to in this lifetime.

This is just a sampling. Many parents would say that their child was making it up or just has an active imagination. What I have found is these experiences are real. They are in tune with their spiritual gifts. They are connected at a spiritual level in which they have memories of past lives, can connect with spirits, talk to angels and ascended masters, see auras, and tap into the all knowing where all information that ever was and ever is exists.

If your child does some of these things, it is not good to ignore it or distract the child out of it. This is part of who they are and they are trying to show you a peek inside of their soul. This is so you know that they can do these things. One should have an open curiosity and ask questions. Ask him what he sees, what he hears, what he knows. Accept it, not as something weird, but more in an interested amazement of what they know and can do. If you fake your interest, they will know, and it may not be pretty. All the children I have met demand our true authenticity and for us to be real. No faking, no appeasing, no distracting away. Unless you want the lesson to come back louder and stronger, that is.

We are fully supported

It can be unnerving to have your child come to you with information that you can't verify. You can't see the hissing cat on the ceiling in his room. You can't see the white spirit with blonde hair in his bathroom. Or maybe you can, but you forgot how to.

One night, my son came running into my room claiming there was a black "demon" dog in his room. He said it had red eyes and was on his bed and he could barely move out of bed. At the time, this type of thing was happening a lot, but I didn't know what to do. I just let him sleep on the floor next to my bed and we talked until he got tired and went to sleep. But the problem was that I "felt" this fear too. I didn't want to go in his room to check it out. I actually was afraid too and I hadn't even seen it. This is because I am energetically sensitive. I can feel things.

The next day I knew I had to do something. I had to figure out how to help us from being afraid when something like this had happened. I called our Naturopath and she came out and worked with us. Through muscle testing she asked certain questions of his subconscious. Even if the mind doesn't know the answers the subconscious does. The answer was that yes, there was a negative spirit in the house. She prayed with Michael and they called in Archangel Michael who is the warrior angel to come and escort this spirit out. She checked and the spirit was gone. They did this for months until Michael no longer felt fear he just "took care of it" himself by working with Jesus and the angels.

It is beautiful to know that we have such amazing beings we can call in for help. Here are a few that I work with most often.

Archangel Michael

He is the protector and warrior angel. You can call him in to put a blue light of protection around your aura. You can ask him to clear out any unbeneficial energy. You can ask him to remove any negative connections you may have for other people. Many children LOVE to have a picture of Archangel Michael in their room. Just the picture alone even if printed off the internet holds a high vibration which is beautiful to have while you are sleeping.

Saint Germain

He is an ascended master that is said to have had many incarnations which have made a huge difference in our world. His special gift is that of the Violet Flame. When we call on Saint Germain and ask to be surrounded in the violet flame we are asking for protection and to transmute (send to the light) any energy that is not in our highest good.

Jesus

Jesus the master healer. I call on him when I need to be comforted, loved and protected. Also, when you need a miracle healing. You will always be answered in one way or another. You may not like your answer but you will always get an answer. I have memories of being in deep grief and Jesus showing up to just hold me. No matter your religious beliefs, he is available to us all.

Blessed Mother Mary

The blessed mother is such a beautiful teacher. She helps us to understand situations based on what the heart says instead of what we hear or think. She commonly says to me, "What does her heart say?" Then I know the answer. She is so helpful when in situations of "he said, she said" where there is conflict. She helps us shift into a loving space of compassion and harmony.

Archangel Metatron

He is with me at all times, in all sessions and is also present with all of the children. His special interest is children with psychic abilities. He helps us on all levels from clearing energy to healing. You know when Archangel Metatron is around if you see shapes and orbs as that is how he works, through the energy of sacred geometry.

Spirit Guides

All of us have spirit guides. These are spiritual beings who have been with us from birth, assigned to help us, give guidance and advice. They never tell us what to do, but they do gently drop signs and hints of the best choice. When we speak to our spirit guides it can often sound like our own thoughts. But when we go deeper, breathe deeper, and relax, we may get a vision of them, or a name, or information as to how we know them. We usually have one or two main spirit guides, along with other guides that come in and out for certain purposes. But we ALWAYS have them with us, so we are never alone.

Archangels and Guardian Angels

We have guardian angels with us just like we have spirit guides. These are not family that has passed, those are more helper spirits. Angels hold a special light frequency that from my experience is 8th dimensional frequencies. Although I reserve the right to change my mind on that as I encounter more lessons and experiences along the way. If you would like to learn more about the Archangels, I definitely would recommend books by Doreen Virtue. There are many other ascended masters and angels you may want to call in and feel connected to. Call in Buddha for peace. Call in Archangel Raphael for healing work. Call in Archangel Gabriel to help with communication. You may have some that you know from your religious beliefs that would be helpful. Just call them in.

You may wonder how you would "call in" any of the above spirits. There must be some special trick, chant, prayer or thing to say. Nope…you just ask. As you come to a more empowered state, you may come to the understanding that we are all connected and ONE. And in light of that, we hold the energy of all of them within us and can utilize this power ourselves. But until that level of awakening happens, just call them. You can say, "Please Archangel Michael clear the energy in his room and infuse it with peace and love." One thing to note is that these spiritual beings are Omni-present. Don't ever feel like you don't deserve to work with one, that someone else may need them more. They are so amazing because they can be many places at once.

Our intention is key though. If you don't believe it's happening, then it isn't. So, call the being you would like, then visualize it happening, see it in your mind, feel it in your body and know that it is being done. It's ok if you feel like you are making it up. Your power of intention is that strong where you can create it and it is real.

Once you understand how beautifully loved and surrounded you and your family are, not only is there a sense of peace, but the vibration in your home raises and the family can be in harmony. Children diagnosed with autism often love a high vibrational environment. Low vibration would include emotions of fear, guilt, and sadness. Who wants to live in that?

Chapter 3:
Bringing the Light into Your Home

One thing that can shift a family out of balance would be the energy imprint we leave behind. Every time you walk in a room, part of your energy continues to exist in that space after you leave. Everything you touch, everything you encounter in any way, leaves an imprint of you behind. This is why many psychics can feel an object and connect with the person or event associated with the object (known as psychometry).

Just as we leave our energy signature behind, we also bring our energetic signature into spaces. Have you ever been sitting in a room and someone else came into the room in a bad mood and you could feel the shift? You may have even felt that mood and then absorbed some of it. You may have become irritable that day as well and not known why. Even our most resilient people are susceptible to this. It is because we are intertwined with each other and affected by energy even if we can't see it or don't intend for that to happen.

So imagine being a child diagnosed with autism and you are ultra-sensitive. Your sensory system is on high alert, yet even more than that, your spiritual antennas are active and pick up on everything. You pick up moods, emotions, and thought processes all from the past, present, and future all at once. It's like watching 200 stations on TV all at the same time! This is what the kids go through on a daily basis. No wonder many appear to be "checked out" and not active and present with us. They eventually tune all of this sensory input out and shift into their spiritual zone.

The spiritual zone is a nickname I have for other dimensions. It's pretty common among parents to hear that their child looks like they are in "another world." We think of it like they are spacing out. But that's actually contrary to what is really happening. If you have ever reached deep meditation or "the zone" you will understanding what I'm talking about. The kids can move into that space easily and effortlessly. It is their comfort zone, where they feel in tune, accepted, loved unconditionally and powerful. They are accessing themselves at their highest spiritual level, living from their soul's divine essence.

In this spiritual zone they may be talking or working with angels. They may be going to many dimensions. Working with ascended masters. Most interestingly, I have found that they are talking to each other. Children who have never met in physical reality are communicating with each other in the spiritual zone, helping each other and each other's families. I am confident that the full reason why I have a busy practice is because of this spiritual communication behind the scenes. The kids talk.

You might wonder, if the kids talk in this "spiritual zone" then how would messages be coming through to parents to do something like make an appointment? This is the amazing part. The kids are such powerful beings, they can send you dreams, ideas and even more kinds of messages throughout your day. Have you ever had an idea just pop into your mind out of nowhere? Have you ever just known what your child wanted to eat without speaking to them? This is their favorite form of communication, telepathy.

The vibration in the spiritual zone is very high. It is one of unconditional love. In this zone, their physical body has no presence, so they feel no pain or uncomfortable feelings. It's only when we make them aware of their body do they jolt back into it and show signs of being uncomfortable.

So how can we help them to be more present with us in the three-dimensional reality which is Earth? We need to make major efforts to raise the vibration in our homes, in us and in people who are around our children. This entire book is really about this, but here are some ideas to get you started.

1. **Recognize the energy you put into the world, into the home.** Are you cranky, frantic, irritable, and easy to snap? You may think it's because of your child and blame it on the stresses of autism. But we are responsible for what we put out. We are responsible for our choices. If you are putting out yuck, then you will receive yuck. It's simple law of attraction which is a Universal Law. You get what you give. So if you want peace and harmony from your child, then you need to make every effort in your life to create that for yourself and infuse that into your world. Your child will benefit directly from your efforts when you work on yourself.

One book I enjoyed was "Zero Limits" by Joe Vitale. He spoke of an ancient Hawaiian healing method called Ho'oponopono. In this healing method we take full responsibility for our thoughts and how we view someone. If you see your child as disabled or having bad behavior that is your choice and responsibility in how you see him. To reverse this process we send these words to our child... "I'm sorry, I love you, please forgive me, thank you." These words have incredible power. If you find yourself falling into a victim mode saying, "but he did this or he did that" then you have missed the point. When you struggle just repeat the phrase over and over if need be. You WILL shift the energy towards the positive.

2. Another thing to understand comes with what we allow. I don't mean allowing behaviors to happen. I mean are we ALLOWING ourselves to shift out of balance, out of peace? Or another idea would be are we CHOOSING this experience?

My daughter is a master of button pushing. If I say yes, she says no, and vice versa, just for the sake of initiating a response in me. She gets plenty of attention so it's not attention seeking behavior. After years of this and finally a pretty tumultuous 6th grade year, I realized I was LETTING her push my buttons. What if there were no buttons to push? What if I chose not to allow myself to respond? I worked really hard on this. She would throw out the jab and instead of responding I would focus on breathing deeply, maintaining balance and a loving heart, then respond. Our interactions have improved a thousand percent since then. I also focused on giving her undivided attention when we are talking, turning my phone over, closing my laptop and just chatting. That small effort brought about big rewards. She still tries here and there to get me riled up, but I am much better and not allowing myself to react.

Not only is it important to understand these interactions and what we allow in our family, but also in our other environments. There are certain things that we are triggered by in our environment that do seem to push our buttons. For me, it is anything about Monsanto, Taiji dolphin hunting, and population control via contaminated vaccines. I'm sure some of you just got triggered by me mentioning these things. You may have felt an increase in your blood going to your head, a tightening of your muscles and your mind saying, "Yeah, yeah, that stuff pisses me off too!" You may have even begun to add to my list. Ok, so let's come back to center and take some deep breaths. If we allow ourselves to be triggered by certain topics, then we are energetically out of balance when we come back in contact with the family.

My suggestion is to decide what your role is here. Can you be involved in advocacy work and stay neutral and balanced? I don't know many that actually can. Actually, I don't know one person that can. But it does seem to go in cycles. One mother can take on the cause and do major work to educate the new mothers, yet then realizes she needs to move on so she can stay in balance more often. And the cycle goes on with another mother moving into that role. It is quite beautiful. What isn't beautiful is if you stay in the advocacy role, remain out of balance most often, and don't move on and let another mother take the reins. I see mothers developing life-threatening illnesses because they haven't nurtured themselves.

Take what I say to heart and look at your individual interactions and group interactions. Are you putting out an energy of peace and love? Or is it anger and victimhood? Just look at it.

A child diagnosed with autism needs our peace and love more than anything else in the world. If you are depleted, then you are unable to give this properly. This should shift into your number one priority above all else. Bringing peace into your world and his, no matter what. You will see really good stuff if you focus on this, I promise.

3. One way to bring the light into your home is to literally call in the light. You can do this through prayer, meditation, and crystals. Allow your child to choose crystals that he likes and place them in his environment. Place pictures of ascended masters and angels that you connect with in the environment. In my home I have spiritual artwork, crystals and icons in my home that my family resonates with. My living room has several amethyst crystals, a large clear quartz crystal, a Buddha fountain and a picture of a beautiful white lion which represents balance of power to me. When I walk in this room I feel connected, at peace and energized with light.

My healing room contains many, many crystals. I have a space for a tribute for my dog Pepper who transitioned last year. It has artwork such as a beautiful mandala, artwork of the seven chakras and a speaker where I put my iPod and often play very relaxing, beautiful music that can emanate to the whole house from that spot.

My family room has a beautiful picture of dolphins swimming, which holds a high vibration of love, joy, happiness, play and telepathy. I also have some dolphin sculpture figurines, a terrarium with plants and crystals that I call the "fairy garden," and a large rose quartz crystal that puts the vibration of love into the room.

Can you see what I'm getting at? Choose things that your child loves, that you love and put those through your home. When you walk in the room you feel that love, your heart opens and your soul feels at home.

I have also set up a special space in the backyard that has this swing chair. I swing in the chair and connect with nature, read and sometimes work with clients from that spot. It helps to ground me and energizes me as well. In that spot, I am at peace.

So I have found things that bring the light into my home. You may not have interest in the things that I love. That is totally fine. But what does make your heart sing? What does your child love? Make a list, and then see how you can infuse these things into your home. You will feel the difference here and when you walk in the room it is like walking home. It's all about creating that sacred space for all to enjoy.

4. You can also do some things to clear the actual energy in the room. Some find these things helpful…

- Essential Oil energy clearing spray. I like the brand Alaskan Essences and their product "Purification." You can find this online at www.alaskanessences.com

- You may also want to learn how to smudge the room. Not everyone enjoys the smell though. This is a Native American tradition in which you burn dried sage and allow it to smoke. You go in a clockwise direction around the rooms furthest from the front door and work your way towards the front door, allowing the smoke to get in all of the corners of the home. Some like to chant or recite the Lord's Prayer as they do this. If you choose to smudge, be sure to just do it calmly and peacefully as if it were another process to cleanse your house. There is no need to feed the fears here.

- You can also cleanse the energy with sound frequency. There is a CD that will do this called Middle Path by an artist named Paradiso. You could play this in the home or room while you aren't in it and allow the frequency of the music to clear the energy. You can listen to it as well and use it during meditation, but it is also an effective room energy cleanser. Other ways would be to use Tibetan Singing Bowls, the Ocean Drum from Remo and Didgeridoo sounds. Of course, not everyone has these sound instruments, so the CD is a good choice.

- If you are attuned to Reiki or any other kind of energy healing, then you may use that frequency to clear the energy in the room as well. Your intention is just as powerful as any other tool. If you are interested in the first level of Reiki, I offer a free course online (at the time of this writing). Just go to www.EpiphanyHealingArts.com and look for the classes.

5. Clear the clutter. Any stacks or piles of stuff is just stagnant energy. Do some spring-cleaning and get rid of that stuff. Consider hiring a Feng Shui expert to guide you on furniture placement for allowing the most lovely energy flow.

Now, as we strive for this more light-filled balanced existence and environment, we may begin to notice other family members and what they are bringing into the home. This isn't going unnoticed to your child either. As much as we want our husband home right after work to give us a reprieve, it is more important that he do some self-monitoring of his energy as well. It is more common that the mother begins to be interested in spiritual practices and the men come later. It's not always the case, I know some men that are leading the spiritual evolution in their home, but that is less common. So, I will speak to the other men, the ones who see their wives going down this path. It is important to be supportive of this in the home as it is best for all. However your part in this is important. Here are some tips for the guys...

- Leave work at work. If your mind is still processing the day then you aren't being present with your family. If you need to do some self-care before returning home then please do that. I suggest going to the gym and releasing your day through physical exercise as something very effective. You can then come home with a clear head and a strong body.

- Emotional release work is important. Your wife isn't the only one grieving and trying to process emotions regarding the health and diagnosis of your child. But I always say, "Better out than in!" Men commonly hold in or hide their emotions as to not add any more emotions to the situation. I totally get that, but in the long run those suppressed emotions turn into physical disease. So, I recommend finding a physical outlet to release those pent up emotions. One method I like is the heavy bag. Get the boxing gloves out and punch that bag. Release anything that you are holding onto that isn't in your highest good. Release frustrations and then take a nice shower to rinse the rest of it all down the drain. Then you can be present and alive and vibrant with your family.

- Active presence is so important. With today's multiple distractions, we are all susceptible to falling into this. While being with your family, turn off the phone, the TV, and the computer and just BE. Over time, you will notice a deeper connection with your wife and your kids. They will appreciate your efforts and you will be happier because you will really be in the family, not just the breadwinner, but you will see how your role here is invaluable.

- Take time to balance and center yourself. Each morning and each evening, take at least 15 minutes and come to center. You can do this through deep breathing, a relaxing shower or just some quiet time to yourself. This time is just for you. When you're done, allow mom to have her time as well, so she can rebalance and realign.

Color

Colors also hold a frequency, a vibration, and can be brought in to harmonize the energy around us. Colors can be seen by clairvoyants in the chakra system, and many colors are associated with the health of the chakra. I see colors as a way of helping understand balance versus blockage or issue in the physical body. Here are some of the common associations with color.

<u>Red</u> – Passionate, excitement, blood, fiery, sexy, intense energy, and associated with the Root or Base chakra.

<u>Orange</u> – Movement, exotic, energizing, initiating action, and associated with the Sacral chakra.

<u>Yellow</u> – Sunshine, happiness, brightening, smiling, joyful, in power, and associated with the Solar Plexus chakra.

Green – Healing, calming, nature, healthy red blood cells, in balance and associated with the Heart chakra.

Pink – Loving, softness, compassion, understanding, gentleness, and associated with the Heart chakra.

Blue – Soothing, water, flowing, effortless easy, calming, peace, and associated with the Throat chakra.

Indigo – A mixture of blue and purple represents clairvoyance, guidance, understanding the deep meaning, inner wisdom, and associated with the Third Eye chakra.

Purple – Divinity, our true spiritual essence, Reiki energy, a flow from divine to self, and associated with the Crown chakra.

White – Encompasses all colors, all that is, overall balance, and divine light.

Black – Lack of any color, blockage, counter balance, clean slate waiting for you to fill it.

Rainbow – A gateway to other dimensions, all inclusive, all loving, in one's power.

You can bring in certain colors for certain purposes. A color frequency is just as powerful as any other frequency if that is the vibration needed to bring in balance. This is why using one's intuition is highest on the list so one can know what is needed and what is not. Also know that any color in excess can shift the balance into imbalance. Intuitively know which to use and which not.

Be mindful of the colors your child wears. If your child is very hyper or intense, you may not want him to where red or orange often. Blue or purple would be a nice choice. So think about how this can come into your daily choices for clothing, artwork, wall colors and more.

There are so many ways you can bring light into your home. Just understand that love is the highest vibration and all we need it. The love you have in your heart and the love you show will infuse the most beautiful light, and your child will feel the power of your unconditional love. This is the love in which it doesn't matter if he speaks or if he reads, it is the love that transcends time. That love will clear the energy better than anything else. That love exists in your soul and is part of you. Your job is to find it and express it for all times.

Chapter 4:
Our Soul's Journey

It's no coincidence that you showed up in this life during this time. Our Mother Earth is at a place of survival. Doesn't that parallel how we feel sometimes in our lives, as if we are just trying to survive each day? Or you can see the beauty in the journey.

As I write this, I am in a beautiful spot in Northern Arizona called Sedona. The area I am in is called Angel Valley and it is known for its high vibration and the space it provides for people to come and shift into a place of unconditional love for oneself. As I journeyed on a little hike today, I came across a beautiful flowing creek. There is a wobbly little wooden bridge with no hand railings that you can use to cross the creek. It takes your full concentration, as the energy is very powerful, and you are almost transported to another dimension. So, staying present was a challenge for me.

As I crossed to the center of the bridge, I looked to the right. On the right side was the powerful flow, almost like a river, running fast over the rough rocks, smoothing them over hundreds and hundreds of years. This rushing flow reminded me of my soul's journey in this life. I am the rough rock, and the water is the rushing experiences that have helped to shape me and evolve. While I was in the rough waters, it wasn't fun, it brought me disease, stress, divorce, grief, anxiety and angry emotions. Yet, even amongst all of that, there were some great experiences as well. As my rock was seemingly "beat up" it was also smoothed and loved and fine-tuned.

As I looked to the left of the bridge, I saw a calmer flowing creek with a gentle current and many beautiful smooth and rounded rocks. This side showed me where I am now and where I will be. This side of the creek was peaceful and flowing with life, with the breeze to go where I am to go. There was no stress, no shaping, no forming, just living in peaceful existence. There are calm waters, soothing energy and gentle movement as I move into this new phase of my life. This is a phase where the rough waters have shaped me but have not defined me.

I find this a beautiful metaphor for our soul's journey. As a parent of a child diagnosed with autism, you may be right in the midst of the rough waters. It's difficult to have the foresight to see the future and if that calm creek is ahead. Know that your journey with this child, with this family is your shaping, your smoothing, and your evolution into knowing who you truly are. And who are you? You are a beautiful, divine, spiritual being living a human life in a human body.

Right now you are being smoothed, fine-tuned and shaped to bring you the awakening to understand who you are. You may think this whole journey is about your child but it is the contrary. It is about you.

This conversation may trigger you to say, "Enough of the rough waters already, I want the peace!" Understandable.

This isn't a journey with a particular destination, though it is a movement that we can all choose to shift into. It's an energetic template that can be brought in as our ultimate creation of who we want to be. My template is healthy, happy, strong, compassionate, connected, present, intuitive, wise and is aligned with her soul purpose, even as it shifts and changes through life. So, anything not supporting that template are things that go outside of the lines for me to acknowledge, love that they exist, and then harmonize them into my template. You can think of it like a random text box showing up when you are writing your Power Point. You can integrate it into the template or you can delete it. But in any event, it needs to be acknowledged. That text box could be a trauma, an emotion, a disease…of course what if that text box enhanced and beautified your template? That would need to be considered.

What does your energetic blueprint, your template look like? This is just for you, not for others. It is important to understand that the only one who you have any power or control over is your own self. You can do all of these things to help your child, but in the end, the choice is his. It is always his choice, his free will. If you find yourself infringing upon free will, then know that you are causing friction energy in both of you. What if you could just let it be?

Make a list of qualities you would like for your blueprint or template of you. It should be general, as I listed in mine. You need to leave an opening for life to happen and for divine timing to bring you blessings that you haven't planned that would spontaneously bring insight and awakenings. This template or blueprint can now become your affirmations, and when you feel yourself shifting out of it, take serious time to meditate to shift yourself back into alignment with it. This is your creation and it is you creating your life, living your soul purpose and aligning with your divine self. When you create this blueprint be sure to always check, "Is this in my highest good? Is it in the highest good for all?" Ultimately, our soul purpose will always serve the highest good for all those around us as well as for us individually.

Part of understanding your soul purpose is to understand that it is not our job to fix anyone else. When we see something that needs "fixing" it is important to look within to see if that something is more about ourselves. Is there a part in us that is triggered by seeing that thing in another, in our child? Does seeing your child in pain make you feel helpless? Does it trigger guilt? Or does it trigger an underlying issue with needing to be the helper or needing to "save" someone. What you envision in the other person is about you. When we see our child as in-jured or harmed then we place them in a victim energy. When we are victims how can we be the victor? We are then immediately locked into polarity...good, bad, evil, light which takes us further from God, Source, Zero Point.

This is where living in the now moment, the present, and being ok, is what we could bring in here. This is where balance, love, compassion, joy, and peace exists in the now moment which is where we are when we are living true to our soul purpose.

The very best thing you can do for your child is to live true to your soul purpose. Live your life in that holy presence. In that space, you set the example, the vibration, and model the human experience so your child can create his own blueprint, just by living in yours with you.

Chapter 5:
The Mind, Body and Spirit Healing Paradigm

Biomedical Interventions

But Why Did That Work for Her Kid and NOT Mine?

One of the biggest issues in the autism community is the inconsistency of results when striving for "recovery" in their kids. What works for some, doesn't work for all. As parents, we look to each other to learn about our experiences. Many feel that doctors have failed them and no longer look to them for all of the answers. So parents spend thousands and thousands of hours online, asking questions, researching and learning scientific concepts that most MD's have no clue about. Some take that knowledge and use it to improve the health of their child substantially, and some do the same thing and see NOTHING.

Ok STOP! I'm not going to pick through protocols, talk about what a parent could be doing wrong or how they must have messed something up. NO! I'm going to zoom out and look at this from a spiritual perspective and share what I have learned working with hundreds of kids diagnosed with autism spectrum, PANDAS/PANS and other labels that lock the kid in a box of status quo.

As an energy healer, I look at the physical body as an expression of the spiritual, emotional and mental bodies. I believe that illness begins in these other energetic fields and when not balanced or harmonized (or energy corrected) works its way in and manifests as a physical reality...an illness, a "disorder," a symptom, a something in the physical body. While sometimes with a direct transmission of an infection, it can be a physical thing but the susceptibility can be tracked back to another source.

For example in a situation of an over population of parasites, one question I would ask would be, "Why do you allow yourself to be attacked?" Many times the answer is something more emotional like, "I don't deserve to be happy. I don't deserve good things." From this vantage point, I would track that belief back to when and why that belief was created. It could be from a past life, current life experience, relationship, etc. When we track it back to the source, the first time this thing was created in the energy field, we can clear, balance and heal that thing.

As I am working with children, I am reading their energy field, talking to their high/low/middle self (via telepathy) and working with their guides, angels and masters for guidance for the family.

As I'm working with these children daily and speaking to them, I'm seeing some clear patterns as to why some are NOT healing at the physical level. (Also referred to as recovery...I prefer healing.)

1. The child doesn't want to heal. They don't see themselves as broken or needing to be fixed. I have had many kids tell me flat out that they can energetically BLOCK any and all treatments that are given to them with the intention of fixing their autism. They ultimately want to be accepted each day and loved unconditionally for the beautiful soul that they are....not our vision or dream of what we wished they would be. When we force anything other than unconditional love, they may feel like their free will is being infringed upon.

2. The child isn't aligned with the treatment or the doctor. Boy this is a big one. I've had a few boys tell me that they are not guinea pigs. They don't enjoy being a trial and error experiment for the doctor or the parent. To some, the INTENTION of the doctor or parents is extremely important. I had one boy share with me exactly why he blocked treatments from a certain doctor. He explained how the doctor had such a big ego and was in it only for the numbers. How many recoveries he had under his belt was his focus. This boy wanted no part in that, and refused to accept anything that doctor put forth. He refused to take the treatment, being combative to his mom. And when she did get things in him he changed the frequency of the item to neutral so that it would do nothing for him.

Other children have shared with me a preference for things that are God- given. Many say they will only take things that are very pure, organic, energetic and beautiful. Anything chemical or pharmaceutical carries a vibration they do not like for their pureness and they reject it. Many children tell me they enjoy energy work, homeopathy, herbs, flower essences, essential oils.

3. Our intentions are not aligned with their soul purpose. This can be a hard one to swallow. Many children who are diagnosed with autism are living for their soul purpose. That purpose may not include living in a healthy body. From my experience with speaking with angels, ascended masters and my own astral travels, meditations and visions, I have learned that before we come into this current body we have a mission. We have a goal of something or things that we want to experience and learn in this lifetime. The soul is always trying to ascend to the next level and by having certain experiences and learning certain lessons we are able to do that. Everyone is different. (Sounds like autism, huh?)

I know in my case that my son is here for a time as a sacrificial lamb. His journey helped me learn a million things I never would have without him. I checked the energy of this. I looked at it before I met his dad. If I had made other choices, gone on other dates, would I have learned these things? The answer is a definite NO. I would have had other experiences but not these. Now that I have aligned with my soul purpose, something shifted. My son stepped out of the autism label and is now no longer a sacrificial lamb, but working on the next phase of his soul purpose. His sacrifice served the purpose for that timeframe and now he's moving on.

Is it possible that your child is this way to teach you? To bring you experiences you would not otherwise have?

What a beautiful gift! Some may think they are unworthy of this, but your soul knows the truth, and as you begin to align with your soul purpose it will all become crystal clear.

4. Divine Timing. This is really connected to number 3 above. But sometimes it's about timing. There is something else that needs to happen before the body can heal. Does he need the energy to be more balanced in the home? Does some lesson need to be learned first? There is a very big example of this that I run into every day. This is about mom.

Our own personal healing is very much intertwined with our children. We are so connected on so many different levels. We even share many physical symptoms with our children. When I was diagnosed with Lyme disease and at the height of my symptoms, I was mute. For one month, I couldn't speak. I became severely sensitive to sound and light where I had to cover my head with a blanket just to be in the family room during the day with the sun shining. I was in pain, I couldn't tolerate many foods and had a severe headache. I was living the symptoms of what many children with autism feel and experience. I wanted to talk, I wanted to scream, but I couldn't. I was frustrated and wanted to hit something or myself. I was given the experience of Lyme disease and those particular autistic-like symptoms for that time so I could UNDERSTAND. So I could EMPATHIZE. So I could LEARN how important my health was too, and not just focus it all on my son. I realize now that I needed to go through this so that I could be a clearer channel to work with the kids. I would've have never guessed that at the time. But looking back, I now know that it was true. It was divine timing.

The very first child I ever spoke to telepathically in my dream said to me, "I need you to help my mom." The kids don't want us to be martyrs for them. They want to heal together and for you to understand your worth and your value. They want you to know your soul, your soul purpose and your divinity. I offer an amazing course for moms and dads filled with inner work and tools on how to connect more deeply with your child. It's called Family Awakenings Course for Awesome Kids, and is available on my website.

5. Intention is EVERYTHING. I've seen this happen over and over again. Mom is afraid to give the treatment. The doctor said he needs it, but something feels weird. They decide to give it anyways because "The doctor must know more than I do" she thinks. So, she gives the treatment and the kid CRASHES. What happened? Two things. First, she gave the treatment with the energy of fear attached to it. Fear breeds fear and nothing good ever comes from it. The fear created what she feared. She worried about him crashing, and energy and thought was put into that reality. The more energy we put into that reality the more it becomes so.

Second, she ignored her intuition. Ouch! Yes, that sounded a little blamey, but it is definitely a very common thing that we all do, every day. Have you ever thought, "Oh, I better take side streets home, there may be traffic on the freeway." Then you didn't. You stayed on the freeway and got stuck in traffic. You kick yourself because you knew better. You just didn't listen. Your intuition is that soft little voice, so quiet and loving, that gently brings you thoughts and ideas. It's easy to overpower with our chatty, loud minds. But our intuition is connected to our spiritual self, which is connected to the divine. So our intuition is divine guidance. It's coming from knowledge from a higher source that knows ALL and the higher source that exists within us.

In the example of giving your child treatment, if something is making you procrastinate giving it, feels funny, or you are fearful of a reaction or that it's not right for him, listen to that voice, that feeling in the pit of your stomach. That, my friend, is divine guidance!

Now on the flip side of this, positive intention in treatments can bring miraculous results. I have been in this autism community for a long time...10 plus years and counting. I've seen a lot of "treatments" come and go. Last year during one of the sessions with an amazing awesome kid, some beautiful guidance came through about autism treatments. This came from beautiful Archangel Raphael who is considered the healing angel.

To summarize, he showed me some of the main treatments that over the years people have said "recovered" their child: GFCF diet, TD-DMPS, MB-12 shots, and most recently the CD Protocol. In each of these treatment protocols a "group mind" was created. This was a group of parents that believed in it, they believed without a shadow of a doubt that if they did this protocol, their child would recover. They believed and spread that belief. Doctors learned it and spread the belief more and more until it was HUGE. Those that locked into this belief were part of this group mind power that amplified the belief and manifested real healing in many kids. But AA Raphael says this was the most powerful part, the group mind power. When the belief began to fade, so did the results people saw. Was it the treatment or the group mind power?

With some of the above protocols I have found that when a parent didn't all the way buy into the belief, the treatment didn't work. So I believe the recoveries are powered by the intention.

You can create this in your home as well. If you are giving your child a treatment that you believe in and you know he is aligned with and wants healing in his body...then infuse that treatment with positive intention. See it going into the body, positively charged with love, exactly what the body needs, doing exactly what it was designed to do and providing results exactly as it is intended, in the highest good for all. Create that group mind power in your own home. Call on the power of a million angels to add to this intention. With prayer, ALL things are possible. Remember...worry is praying for what you don't want. So reverse that and intend for what you DO want.

6. Improvements are connected only to speech. Ok, so speech may have been lost due to a regression via environmental insults, but it may not redevelop for other reasons. I talk to parents every day that are gauging their child's improvements based on whether they are speaking or not. Sometimes it's just not that cut and dry.

Here are some of the things kids have told me over the years about speech...

- "I can teach more from a place of silence. My silence allows others to develop their gifts in order to understand me."

- "It's not time...I want to speak eventually but more things need to be done before I'm ready to allow that to happen."

The truth is that the body can make many improvements and the speech not change one bit. I recently took a class from Hector Garcia in which he said that it takes a 65% change for us to track the change. So if our gut heals only by 50% we may not feel or notice it as much, but when it hits that 65% improvement milestone we KNOW we had improvement. Sometimes valuable treatments are getting dumped because no speech was seen. But improvements very well may have been made.

7. The energy or dosage of the treatment is wrong. Learn to muscle test! This is the most valuable tool out there to fine tune things. You can muscle test anything it just needs to worded in a yes/no question. Some will do this with a pendulum, also called dowsing. Or you can learn one of the many muscle-testing techniques. I used to always talk about how important muscle testing is, but parents didn't have resources to learn or know how to do it. So, I created an online muscle testing class. You can watch the recording of one of the classes called Muscle Testing Made Easy on my website. You can find it at http://www.epiphanyhealingarts.com/Muscle_Testing_M ade_Easy.html. With my son, we tracked that his body would shift every two weeks. So every two weeks we needed to adjust his treatment and dosages. When we stayed on top of this, he made the most improvements. You can also pay someone to muscle test for you, but I believe it's better to learn the tool yourself so you can use it anytime, anywhere.

8. Locked in the box of the label. A diagnosis is a curse. Yep that's right. It's an energetic curse and unless we transmute that curse it becomes who we are. Just as if we are called stupid enough times in our life, we act stupid. We live the belief. If we believe we are autism or our child is autistic, then he is. It's energy. It's manifested. So one thing I do in sessions is track the energy of the label. How many people "believe" this child has or is autism. Then I clear that energy from the energy field. He no longer needs to hold that. He no longer is that. He is now free to BE himself and whoever he wants to be. He is no longer locked in that box. This is also related to our be-liefs. Do you believe autism is a bad thing? If you believe that and your child is labeled that then you believe he is a bad thing. Can you be neutral to the word autism? If so, then you have just given no charge to the label of autism. You have taken away any negative and any positive power from the term. That is the neutrality and the goal. So if someone else refers to your child as autistic it won't matter because the word has no power, it is just a series of letters and sounds.

This goes for any "label" like hyper, angry, aggressive, sad, stupid, retarded, etc. Release the label and release them from needing to be this way. When I made a conscious effort to refer to autism in the past for my son, big things happened! When I stated publicly I no longer had Lyme, I didn't. I put my belief into freedom to be who I wanted to be and that's what happened. The same is true for my son. Look at your child...who are they? Do you see only autism? Or can you see the beauty, the wisdom, the intuitiveness, the amazing awesomeness that is your child? Look deeper. Look! If you were your child's angel and could only see good...what would you see? Help him manifest who he really is. See it, know it and believe it!

Lastly, I want to just add that there are probably many more reasons here yet to be revealed. Staying open to these possibilities is the first step. There is still lots to learn.

Emotions and Traumas

Even though most of us try to leave the past in the past, there is still an energetic imprint left from emotions and traumas. Sometimes, this is a cellular memory and held in the physical body. Other times it is held in our soul or other levels such as our mental or emotional fields. This is why when triggered by something, these old energies can be brought to the surface and rise up as if they are asking to finally release and clear.

Children are no different from adults, they also experience this same thing. We all can hold old emotions even from in utero. If it was an unexpected pregnancy and abortion was considered, that child might have imbedded memory of this and even wonder if they are truly wanted, thoughts of wondering if they were a mistake could enter into their mind. People spend years in talk therapy working through these past traumas, when in fact can be handled much quicker through good energy healing.

If you are the type that wears your emotions on your sleeve, then your child will likely pick up on these and show them back to you. That means they would act out these emotions as well. You might feel that this is because of your strong connection to your child and you are "alike." But it is more that they are bringing this pattern to your attention for you to learn to balance these emotions.

Emotions are not bad. Emotions are totally human and a necessary beauty of life. Each emotion serves a purpose, even anger, rage and disgust. We may not always know what that is in the heat of the moment. But if you choose to look and find clarity you will discover it. Other emotions such as joy, happiness, and love are beautiful emotions and when we focus on infusing those emotions into our world, choosing to be those emotions, other emotions just don't seem to have the impact that they did in the past.

As adults we have choices, but the children also have choices. They may feel disempowered and don't understand that it is their choice to choose joy. But they do have the choice. You can model to your children through your own choices. Show them that although you used to get mad on the freeway during traffic, it's ok now because that gives you more time in the car together to listen to music, or to sing or to just be together. You can make that choice. When you make that choice, it opens up space for your child to feel empowered to choose as well.

In energy work, one can track the core cause of the emotion and go to the heart of the issue rather quickly and balance and harmonize that energy with frequency. The same can be said for traumas, whether past life or current life. Those traumas can be traced back to the event and healed from that perspective. It is very effective, and can really bring a lot of relief to the client as it is no longer a burden they need to carry.

Emotional balance does not mean hiding the old crotchety emotions. It means we have come to terms with those emotions. We own those emotions as part of our experiences in life. And we are in balance with them. We don't let them control us nor do we control them. They exist and we exist in harmony together.

Mental Mindset and Perception

One day, I was working with a boy and he told me something profound. He said to me, "Tears are just releasing what's stuck." Yes, that made sense, tears are an emotional release, a form of clearing. Then I said to him, "What about when a toddler is having a temper tantrum, what's stuck?" He replied, "His mindset!" Why, yes that's true. Boy, can our mindsets get stuck sometimes. We pick up on beliefs in many places. When we are little, we take on the beliefs of our parents. When we are in high school, we pick up on the beliefs of our teachers and friends. When we are in our 20's we pick up on beliefs from our friends and co-workers. We pick up on beliefs from TV, movies, the news, radio and of course the internet. If we pick up on these beliefs, how do we know what is really ours?

I have seen an emerging pattern coming through the autism world. It is the shedding of the belief "Doctor knows best." Many have felt that their child was harmed by going with the flow of the mainstream pediatrician. The feeling like they gave their power to make choices up to the doctor and got screwed in the end. There is a huge shift going on with this where people are taking their power back and learning healing methods they can do at home. Many only use holistic methods and do very well with this. We feel that we have somehow reached outside of the box and are free of that old way. Here is the clincher. I've seen a few families where lately they were so into the holistic way that when their child really did need mainstream medical care, it was extremely difficult for them to go there. They avoided it at all costs. Is it possible that by shifting into a holistic model, we only put ourselves into a different box? Being free of a box would mean that whatever is in the highest good of the person would be what you would do, whether it be holistic, mainstream, woo-woo, or whatever. That is true freedom.

There are many treatment protocols that have the "my way or the highway" approach. I take the highway, thank you, because there is no one-size-fits-all solution for any child. This is an absolute statement and I stand by it because I know it to be the truth. What works for one doesn't work for all. I just gave you an example of a mindset that I have. It is when you have a belief that you are unwilling to waver from.

We see this stuck mindset a lot in our families. One example I can give you for myself is about food. I eat a vegan, gluten-free lifestyle. When I found a vegan place that served gluten-free/vegan lasagna, I nearly lost my mind! When I had my first piece, it tasted like heaven. It was the best tasting lasagna I had ever had. The next week, I dragged my husband an hour away to go back to the same place to have another slice of that ooey gooey lasagna. Well….they were out. The monster-sized tantrum I had could have competed with the most stubborn of toddlers. That included a bad Yelp review. Boy was my mind set! Does this sound familiar to you? Does your child do this? Do you do this?

How do we deal with a stuck mindset? As an adult, we can have our little tantrum and then bounce back from it. But the kids aren't quite as quick to recover. The first step is understanding. Imagine that you can put your awareness in your child's body, in their mind, in their shoes. What are they feeling? How is this affecting them? When we understand from their point of view, we can bring compassion to the situation. If we sit in judgment and think about how annoying the behavior is, then good luck with that, because more of those behaviors you will have. The children really just want to be heard and be understood. You don't need to fix the situation and be the savior, but you can be the soft pillow to land on with your compassionate and understanding heart. This leads me to the next topic, perception.

In a beautiful meditation, I was shown that every event, everything that happens, has multiple perspectives, even as much as 16 perspectives or more. We as humans tend to just see our perspective. If you are an empathetic person you may see two or three. But what if you could see all perspectives and take in that information? It makes that saying "there are two sides to every story" look narrow-minded.

How to apply this in daily life is always the challenge. Let's take a sample issue. You are in Target and your child grabs candy off the shelf and when you try to take it away he pitches a huge hissy fit.

Sample perspectives:

Mom: I'm horrified, everyone is staring, why does he have to do this and embarrass me?
Kid: That candy looks so good I have to have it!
Kid's digestive system: Feed me, feed me.
Kid's pancreas: I need sugar to balance me right now.

Kid's brain: I am getting really cranky and need something to help me.

Other people: Oh wow, he is upset.

Cashier: Oh, this happens all the time.

Can you see how looking at multiple perspectives can give you deeper understanding? With using our own perspective alone, we move into a victim mode along with some anger. But looking at many perspectives brings a clearer picture. If you saw these multiple perspectives, would you change any part of your reaction to the situation next time?

I challenge you to look at your own beliefs and release the ones that don't serve you anymore. If you release them, then your children are less likely to pick up on them and carry them as their own. After all, isn't this how prejudice and bigotry stayed alive for so many generations? It took brave ones to shift out of that mindset and look into their hearts for the answers, and our world is much better because of it.

Family Patterns and Genetic Mutations

It is very interesting how many things that we carry aren't ours or didn't originate with us. Have you ever been labeled something in your family? For example, "Oh, she's the stubborn one." "Oh, she gets that from her dad." It is often talked about in families how personality characteristics are passed down through the family. But what if we could get rid of those? Do you have to be stubborn just because your dad was? It feels like many of

:ked into these patterns from birth. These pat-
...e it difficult for us to be independent in who we
are, and make us question who our true self is.

In the awesome children, they can also hold family patterns in their energy field that help to shape some of their
behavior, just like we do. We can track certain behaviors
as family patterns and when we find the relative that this
pattern started with, it can be cleared, and all within that
pattern can benefit from it. Here are some examples of
family patterns...

- Stubbornness

- Difficulty speaking up for oneself

- He's a yeller

- Never says he's sorry

- He can never admit when he's wrong.

- Addiction behavior

Of course, there are lots of beautiful things we can get
through family patterns as well. Let's not forget about
those. The cutting edge work right now is all about epigenetics. Our genes can express mutations and cause a
whole host of issues in the physical body from impaired
detox to difficulty absorbing Vitamin D. Epigenetics is all
about finding what causes genetic mutations to express
and cutting it off at the pass. The work of Amy Yasko and
others is groundbreaking for determining what supplements and dietary changes can be used to alter the expression of these genes.

But what about energy work? Everything is energy, and so are our genes. I like to track the genetic mutations back to its source of creation. When was this mutation created in the family line? With whom did it start and why? I'm finding that deep in our family lines are traumatic experiences. That trauma has caused the gene to mutate in this way. Some examples I have found are famine, plague, other diseases, torture, prejudice and more as some of the things our ancestors dealt with that altered their genes. Those genes in their altered state were then passed down the line to our children.

My working theory is that if we energetically clear the trauma that started the mutation, we can alter the energy of the expression through the descendants. You can also ask what is needed so this mutation will not express. It's not always a supplement, it can also be different forms of energy work. When you work with someone who is in spirit to help clear something from their physical life, it can have a domino effect to all of those affected by that trauma indirectly. So indirectly, healing is happening for the entire familial line.

Karma, Past Lives and Metaphors

Karma is a principle that most of us have heard of. It is usually referenced in Eastern religions, but the concept of Karma is not foreign to Christians. The concept is that what you put out in the world, you get back. So, if you do something bad in your life, something bad will come to you. Kind of like "You reap what you sow." What I have learned about Karma is that it is not just affected by this life. We incarnate with familiar souls and can therefore have Karma in our current relationships that have nothing to do with today. Karma isn't God punishing you. It's a Universal Law that exists to bring everything to balance eventually.

Karma isn't just bad, it's also good. The more good we put in the world, the more we good things we are given. We don't get to actively choose any of this. The Universe works it out.

Sometimes the kids are impacted by Karma in their current lives. It's always possible that they have a Karmic debt, which would mean that to balance some bad deeds, they need to do good things in this life. I just bring this up not to get into detail but just to show you that this is an option of something to consider.

Past lives are very much an issue for the children. One teacher I know talks about how children diagnosed with autism are a "new race" who have never incarnated on Earth and come from star beings. I have not found this to be true in this same way.

What I have found is that the children do have past lives. They have had many on Earth, but also in other Universes. Some may not have been in an Earthly body recently, which makes it difficult for their energy body to acclimate to a dense physical body, while others have had thousands of lives on Earth. One thing is clear though, that these are not new souls. These are souls with a connection to deep wisdom from the past, present and future. Some may even be ascended masters, while others hold an angelic frequency. Does that make them better than the rest of us? Of course not, because we are all God's creations and all hold the light frequency of God. Some of the kids have just had more lives, more mastery and have a higher vibrational frequency than we do. However, with such beautiful beings in our own home, it's no wonder we are called to the spiritual path at one time or another for ourselves. They are calling us, or often dragging us kicking and screaming. But at least we are finally starting to get it.

Even children with past lives who hold an angelic frequency can have Karma from past lives. Anything is possible, and anything can be cleared, healed and loved if it is in the highest good and aligns with their soul purpose.

I mention metaphors because sometimes we will get a vision of a past life but it wasn't an actual past life. Spirit loves to communicate through metaphors, so we will really examine and connect to get the full answer. This is just something to be aware of.

Chapter 6:
Viewing Your Child through a New Lens

Much of what I am asking you to believe is based on my own experiences with the children. When I work with a child, I come from a neutral place, a place of unconditional love, where I honor their journey and thoughts. When the child is your own it's not always easy to come from that place. After all, you are the one getting the behaviors or seeing him appear to be in pain. You are in his 3D physical reality, I am not. I am in a multi-dimensional reality with the child. That is the space where healing can be done most beautifully. But it is also a place where one can see the truth from all perspectives.

Spherical Vision

One way to think of this vision is a technique called spherical vision. This method, taught to me by German Energy Medicine Pioneer, Uwe Albrecht, is very effective. In this method, you imagine that you are in the center of a sphere. You imagine that you can see the situation from all angles, left, right, top, bottom, outside, inside and so on. In this way, we see life from the big picture perspective instead of just ours, which is filled with our judgments based on our experiences. You may zoom and not see the details, but only the energy field of the situation. This may take some practice, but when you look at things in this way you get the intuitive answers closer to the truth of the situation, without preconceived ideas or judgments.

Blessed Mother Mary

Another technique was taught to me during a meditation from our Blessed Mother Mary. She came through to me with a simple phrase that stuck with me and I use today when I feel I have taken sides or shifted into a single perspective (my own). She said to me "Read their heart, what does the heart say, what was their intention." Wow! When you move into a space where you can do this, you will be amazed at what you can find out. Most times, I have found that what I felt were ill intentions weren't. It was someone just trying to do the best they could do. Most people and children do not intentionally set out to make your life miserable. They are just doing their best to manage their life. So when you find yourself in a "he said she said" episode or feel in counter balance with another, read their heart.

Archangel's Teachings

Working with the Archangels is also a beautiful way to see life and situations through another lens. Here is a technique you can use. Imagine that you are that person's guardian angel. As his guardian angel, what does he feel, what does he know, what would you like to see for your person? I have found that when you view the person from the eyes of an angel, your ability to love and hold compassionate space increases dramatically. One is much more able to deal with day to day shenanigans when you come from this viewpoint. An angel understands divine timing and that not all progress happens on our 3D time-line. If it did, then we would be controlling everything and that isn't what we are here for. If your life is lived this way then surely awakenings are coming your way.

Viewpoint of Your Higher Self

Not only are we able to use these beautiful ways of view-ing situations, but you can also move into the viewpoint from your Higher Self. Many people teach that the Higher Self is also the Soul. Some don't believe this. I will leave it up to you to experience and make your own choice. In either event, it doesn't matter. We all are living a life of multiple dimensions. We aren't just a physical body. We are also an energetic field with multiple layers and multi-ple selves. When we intend to see or understand from this higher perspective, I am speaking of the place that is from our all-knowing, our soul level in which only love exists. When we move into that space, we can get a whole new perspective on life and individual situations because from that place is only love and compassion. You will know without a doubt that you are receiving information from that space. It is unmistakable because you will feel it deep in your heart.

Dropping Into Your Heart

Sometimes we are just so up in our heads. Our mind gets running a mile a minute and if you are having an issue with your child, you may not always respond with loving vibes. One technique I learned was to drop into your heart. When your head is going, going, going, try this....

1. Take 10 deep breaths.

2. Observe that you have thoughts but see those thoughts floating on by. (Like an airplane pulling a sign.)

3. Then, focus your breath and attention to your heart. Imagine it is your heart breathing in and out, in and out.

4. Feel the love you have for yourself in your heart. Breathe in and out, in and out.

5. Feel the love you have for your child in your heart. Breathe in and out, in and out.

6. Now bring your attention to the situation while still feeling your heart, breathe in and out, in and out.

7. What do you feel in your heart about the situation? Before responding, be sure it is coming from your heart and not your mind. If you feel your mind popping in, just keep breathing until you are in balance and can move forward from a place of love and compassion.

All of these techniques raise your vibration as a parent. When you raise your vibes then your child can more easily harmonize with your energy. When you are in harmony life is much, much sweeter.

Chapter 7:
Underlying Meanings of Behaviors

When you're in the 3D world and not looking at things through a new lens, it may be difficult to determine why a child is doing a certain thing. Why is he aggressive, why is he pacing, etc.? Our experience with autism specialists and therapists lead us to always look for the physical cause. I've heard so many times "It must be yeast." Or if he's banging his head, "It must be gut pain." And yes, sometimes it is, but sometimes it's not. Sometimes, and in my experience most times, it is something totally different. The emotions that a child has are not always obvious to the rest of us and are often underneath the surface expressing themselves in ways that we don't express them as adults. The verbal expression is one of the primary ways in which we express our feelings, emotions and thoughts. But if a child has not developed that verbal expression, then they find other ways to communicate hoping that we will "get it." Do we get it?

I am going to do my best here to explain some of the common behaviors and what I have learned can be underneath the surface at play as a potential cause of these behaviors. It's not an all or nothing kind of thing. My intention here is to open you up to the possibility that more is happening than meets the eye.

Aggression

Aggression is a tricky little bugger. Yes, sometimes it does have a physical cause. But does that physical cause stem from a physical thing, or before that physical thing manifested is there an energetic piece? Energy workers believe that all issues start outside the body in the energy field. They work through the mental, emotional, spiritual bodies that are unseen to the naked eye. They go through these layers until manifesting physically. So often what is seen as physical started way before that, with some sort of emotional or mental process, sometimes at the soul and spiritual level as well. So it's important to understand that when talking about this subject.

Many of my wonderful clients have had or do have issues with aggression. Here are some of the things that have been the underlying cause...

Head banging: Beliefs and emotions such as, self-hatred, everyone hates me, I do everything wrong, etc.

This also applies to self-injurious behavior like hitting oneself in the head. Often times the child feels like since he is constantly corrected for this behavior or (like in ABA methods) that he can't do anything right. He feels worthless and is deeply hurt. He also may feel like he is a burden. If the parents complain about how bad their life is either silently or out loud, oftentimes the child will show it in this self-injurious behavior. Please understand that you don't need to be in the same room with your child in order for them to hear you or know your thoughts. He can read you like a book, you can be sure of that. If you find yourself hating your life, hating autism in which your child has been labeled, they think you hate them. It is confusing to them because you may give tons of love and then on the other side have these feelings. This up and down cycle breeds imbalance in both parent and child. This is another situation in which working on yourself as the parent can cause monumental shifts of peace in your child.

Attacking others: Here are some of the things that have shown to be related to this...

- The person being attacked has underlying anger and the child is mirroring that anger through their behavior.

- The person is thinking negative thoughts about the child and it feels invasive or even attacking towards the child and they retaliate.

- The child is in fight or flight mode and is having an underlying emotional response that is a reflection of the immune system's response to an invader. In this instance a two prong approach is needed....uncover the physical issue and work on the emotional piece.

- The child is extremely energetically off balance. He may have negative spirit attachments that are in control of his behavior. It is important to hold a very neutral ground in this situation. Show the utmost of balance and neutrality as you need to hold a space of calmness. Do not let fear come in and amplify the situation. If a child is allowing this kind of thing to happen, then there is some deeper soul level work that needs to be done with a qualified Shaman or Energy Healer.

- The child may be trying to teach a lesson. It is unfortunate that some choose violence to teach lessons, but it is a fact. What kind of message would one be sending through this type of behavior? Is he teaching you to "stand your ground," or to call in for Angelic assistance, or maybe to allow him to express himself? The types of lessons here can be endless. Many times our most valuable lessons come from what seems like the darkest of events or places.

We will talk about techniques that can be used to help in these situations in following chapters. My intention was to just open your mind to other possibilities in regards to what could be going on during these aggressive acts.

Pinching and poking: This is related to wanting your full presence.

With all of the technology, social media and our multiple-devices we are more than ever NOT present with our family. Kids find new ways all the time of trying to get us to drop these and really be present, an active participant socially in their lives. I have a friend who just posted a few days ago that her son tried to flush the iPad down the toilet, and then a few days later tried to flush her iPhone. I believe he is sending a message and showing us an example of how a behavior can have underlying meaning and be a communication, an important communication for those around him.

Stimming

Stimming, short for self-stimulatory behaviors, can show itself in many ways. It can be anything from pacing to repeating certain words or phrases to tearing up paper over and over. It's really anything that the child does over and over and hyper focuses on. It is thought to provide comfort to the child. Yet, if we view it through another lens there may be some other reasons or purposes for stimming.

- Stimming can be grounding for a child. It can help them to balance their energy and be more "in" this world. Or, it can be the opposite...they feel more comfortable detaching from this world so stimming provides the monotony to allow for that detachment.

- Stimming can be a tool they use to organize their thoughts. To bring the thoughts solidly in their mind so they can use them later.

- Stimming can be used to balance their emotions. If he is emotionally distraught he may use this as a tool to bring his emotions into balance.

- Vocal stims may be a form of energy healing. I have physically witnessed children making humming, groaning or screeching noises repeatedly. One boy was humming and to some may have been annoying. But to me, I swear I heard him humming OM. It was so soothing and loving, I said to him, "I know what you are humming and thank you." He gave me a wink and a smile and then went back to humming. Screeching can be another form of energy healing. In sound healing and in tribal medicine these sounds have been used to match the energy frequency of an imbalance. Sometimes when you match it, it releases and changes. So really, he could be clearing energy.

In my private practice I have been known to do vocal toning in certain situations with clients. In one instance, this woman had an imbalance in her liver. I was spiritually guided to match the sound of the imbalance. It was a low, guttural, disgusting sound which brought my dogs into the room staring at me sideways. When I was complete, she felt much better and her liver was in balance.

Finger Flicking and Tapping

Oh, this is my favorite! I didn't truly get this one until I was at the Autism One conference in 2013. I was in our booth and a beautiful young girl named Kaitlyn came by with her mother. She jumped up on the massage table and began grabbing my hands to put them places on her body, for me to balance her energy. She was telepathically telling me that her tummy hurt and she was really having a hard time. She then began flicking her fingers. I asked her what she was doing and she said, "I'm helping you balance the energy in here." Ah, of course, I thought to myself. When I am doing a distant healing with a client I often flick my fingers and move my hands in odd ways as I am working and harmonizing the energy field. She was doing the same thing! To the untrained eye, this may look like a self-stimulatory behavior or lack of control of motor skills. But to me it was energy work.

Kids also tell me that they may use tapping in the same way. They may be moving energy, harmonizing or just enjoy bringing that sound into the world.

Meltdowns

When a child has a meltdown, it is a release. It is a purging of emotions that have piled up within him. It may be all his emotions or also those he picks up from others around him. But really this explosion is a huge release.

Non-Compliance

A child that is non-compliant typically indicates one that has an issue with control. They either want to be in control or rebel because they do not want to be controlled. Many of these beautiful ones are highly evolved beings and it may be difficult to be in a body in which one is not able to be the Master. You never know, your child may have been a King in a past life. One with that kind of masterful energy may have a difficult time doing anything anyone wants of them. This balances out over time but looking at control issues in the child or as a family pattern of behavior is the place to go with this. Giving choices so the child feels in their power is a good solution. This control issue may also be a mirror issue. (See below.)

Tracking Energy

This may not be visible to you but I have seen kids taking their finger and pointing to things, looking at things in the air or something else. Energy tracking is simply following the energy. It can be about anything. They may be tracking your thoughts. Tracking the cause of their headache or the cause of your headache by touching your head. It is really limitless. Think of how a tracking dog can find an item or person miles away because they follow the scent. Energy has a "scent" so to speak and one that is tuned in to this can track that energy. The energy can be anything you can imagine. In energy healing, we track the core cause of an issue. We may see and understand just the current symptom but when you track it back, you go on a whole journey to uncover the cause and when you find the cause you have already found the cure. The kids do this.

Mirroring

In spiritual circles, you may hear that everything in life is a mirror, everything is a reflection of our own selves, our beliefs, our emotions, our issues. The logical mind doesn't really want to buy that. We want to reject that because then it puts into question all that we believed to be true. My mind doesn't want to accept it. I started experimenting though. Since I have a pre-teen daughter, I had the perfect subject. Last summer, I decided that whenever she annoyed me I would look at what she was doing and see if that existed within myself. I found that nine times out of ten it WAS about me. Sometimes the lesson isn't about an active issue you have, but it may be a reflection of the worst part of you or the best part of you.

The best part of me is loving and empathetic and really connects deeply with animals. I see that my daughter has this quality and reflects it out into the world. It is part of me too.

The worst part of me is selfish and lazy with a trigger temper (luckily not so much anymore.) There are times when my daughter shows me this exact thing and even stronger than mine at times.

Is this her or me? I believe it's both. But sometimes it is to show me that I need to work on something. If her temper comes out of nowhere, I can look at myself to see if I have been doing that lately. If I have, then it's time for some inner-work. If she is acting extra lazy, I can look to myself to see if I am doing the same thing. It may be time for me to change up my energy a bit and get some work done. I can shift the mirror lesson by changing my behavior and what I noticed is that her behavior changes too!

We may think that we are the parents, the teachers here, but life shows us a different story. These children here have come into our lives not just to be our kids and learn from us, but to teach and help us as well.

Energetic Expression (showing the chaos, etc.)

Children and adults diagnosed with autism commonly express the energy around them. If there are lots of people and lots of excitement in the room they may show that energy in their behavior by pacing, dancing, jumping, screeching, or something similar. If someone comes in the room angry, he may become angry as well.

These kids are energy matchers. If you are joyful, he may show joy in his behavior. If that expression is negative, then to the untrained eye this looks like sensory issues. But when you understand that this is energetic sensitivity, you can either change up the energy in the room or remove him from the environment. This is why sensory breaks work so well.

I have also noticed with myself that if I wear a cap or beanie the sensitivity to energy is muted and it is easier to manage in times of chaos.

How to tell if it is physical illness causing the behaviors

For decades, doctors have been telling moms that if their child has excessive giggling, then it is an overgrowth of yeast in the intestines. They have also been saying that if one is head banging, they have digestive issues. It is pretty much always blamed on the digestive system. Yes, it can be the digestive system. But can also be one of the above things we talked about. So how would you know the difference?

The truth is that issues can contain many layers. There may be an emotional layer, a mental mindset, family trauma, and a physical issue all as part of that one behavior. Luckily, if we work on the first layers like the emotional or mental level, the physical body is realigned to be able to heal itself. It is always good to look through that spherical vision to be able to feel and know what truly is going on. Muscle testing can help you to prioritize your suspicions of the cause and can be used as a gateway to the subconscious where all information is known. If there is one thing every person should know, it is muscle testing. It is the beginner's way to find information without costly, invasive lab testing. It is quick, easy, and a great tool to use until you gain confidence in your own intuition.

Chapter 8:
Messages from the Kids

The most beautiful gift I have to offer is the gift to connect parents to their children. This gift comes through the ability to channel messages from the child to others. I am honored to share these messages from a few of my young friends. Please note that the names of the children have been changed because often times their messages are so profound that people want to connect with them energetically. This is not always in their highest good, so I have changed the names due to this reason. Just connect to their words and their messages and you will feel the love in them.

A Message from Jeffrey

I've grown up and been so alone in my mind for so long. But one day, I felt understood. It was the day I saw the light. I saw my own light for the first time. I couldn't believe that was me. I felt like I had been lost in my own little world, but the truth was that I just didn't see. I was only seeing my perspective, but then when Tami said I had this light shining within me, it's like I saw a picture of myself and there I was. I was a spirit being. I was full of light and I could do good things. I practiced every night while I was in bed. I held my head up so I could stay awake a little later and I waited. Angels surrounded me and I could be in heaven but also be here. In that space, I learned so many things, like how to heal cancer, how to heal myself and how to let things go, sometimes for the greater learning of others around me. It's not easy because you watch people you love suffer and I can sometimes know the greater reasoning. But when it all comes together, I see such an enormous happiness inside me and inside my mom that I can't help but chuckle out loud and show her how happy I am and how loved I feel. If I could say one thing to all the parents out there it would be to SEE your son. They know you so deeply and may have gotten angry or fearful and disconnect from you. It's not because they don't love you, it's because they are learning how to be in their body. Their body may not feel comfortable. They are used to being a spirit and the body is so harsh, it hurts sometimes, so it's easier to detach where there is no pain into our more spiritual selves. I used to do that all the time.

They also may feel stress coming from you. They want to be at peace and happy and stress around them can hurt them. The only thing to do is work on your own life and come to peace with your life and how it is right now. If you resist your life then you resist the lessons that come with it and all of this would have been for nothing. Our experience on Earth is for learning and for loving. If you resist both then all the work by those around you is lost. The other thing I want to say is that I have more choices than you think. I decide when I want to say something or when I don't.

There was a time when speech was taken from me due to physical circumstances...but now that I am awakened I see my choice in the matter and how that experience brought a lot of richness of experiences to me and an incredible amount of learning and compassion to those around me. I wouldn't change that. If I could go back to the time before I regressed and decide to keep my speech, I wouldn't. Most don't realize it but someday you will see all that was accomplished by that one sacrifice on my part. It's mind-boggling. The most important thing you can do as a parent is to LOVE UNCONDITIONALLY. Not to fix things in your child. When you LOVE TRULY AND PURLY you open up the space for miracles to come. Step back and see the beauty!

Tami…tell them your mantra. (My mantra I use here and repeat over and over to raise my vibration and to help me align and put love into what I do.)

I am love
I am light
I am joy
I am peace
As I heal
Others heal
As others heal
I heal
We are ONE
In Divine Light

A Message from Joey

"I know what my job is. It is to raise the vibration of all around me. I take this very seriously. I know what to do to become a regular boy. When I feel my job is complete I will do that. Here are the things I need my family to do...

1. Shed the old traumas.
2. Forgive themselves and others.
3. Understand their energy and the power of their words.
4. Be authentic.
5. Lead with your heart...always.
6. Feel deep compassion for ALL beings.
7. Not trying to mold me into something that YOU want.
8. Nobody should be a martyr for me (take time to take care of yourself too).
9. See life through His eyes.
10. See the beauty of life.
11. See my spirit self.

A Message from Samuel

I very much have much to be grateful for in this life. I have overcome many struggles both with my physical body but also with my spiritual self. You see, I am at odds with two realities. The reality that I am in a strange place with strange people, called Earth. And that I am with loving people whom I have chosen to live this journey with but am away from my comfort zone which could be called "heaven." So, I sometimes veer back and forth between two worlds and at times feel part of neither. But at other times feel fully accepted and empowered in both. It's a tough one, isn't it?

I want to share something with parents in hopes that you will understand your child more deeply. Your child is amazing! He may have been labeled "special" but that word has taken a negative connotation these days. It wasn't intended to be, so I prefer amazing." Your child is able to connect to other children through a portal in their mind that takes them to their energy body, in spiritual dimensions, where he is vibrant and healthy. In this spiritual dimension much good work is being done. Many are setting up communication networks to bring higher-level teachings to the world. One of the ways I found Tami was through this communication network. She was named an ambassador for our purpose and many children and spiritual beings worked to create opportunities for her to do this. Experiences were brought to her for her to learn more. People were put into her life to teach her or for her to teach. This is just one example of how these communication networks can create.

This is also used within our own families. Have you ever heard that saying that if that "thing" comes in your awareness three times you should pay attention? How do you think that "thing" gets in your awareness three times? It is a spiritually guided process and that happens in these higher spiritual dimensions with kind souls working together to create and manifest this in three-dimensional reality, also known as our world.

It is not just those diagnosed with autism that participate in this communication network. We all do and play some role in it, whether we are the messenger or the receiver, we all participate. Also, many on this Earth that are "old souls" and have much spiritual experience who partici-pate in this as well. I cannot leave out our animal spirits that are no different than our spirit. The only difference is what physical form they inhabit, they are still beautiful divine beings like you and I. They also play a huge role in moving humanity to a higher frequency, a place where love and compassion are at the forefront of our existence.

I bring all of this up because in your home you may hear your child mention the name of another child, possibly your friend's child whom he has never met in person. You wonder how he would even know anything about this child. As I explained, this is how.

Lastly, I want to say that I hope you have an understand-ing now that there is much, much, more than meets the eye with the children. Next time you see your child, think of what I say and see what you feel.

A Message from James

I write to you with a message about your child's essence. These children come to this Earth to teach, to love, to shift and to evolve to their next spiritual level…like another notch on their spiritual belt. They are looking for ascension too and as they provide this service in our world they ascend to the masterful level in their own journey. So, although they are helping humanity, so much to awaken to their own gifts, you are helping them as well by providing a safe haven for them to do their work. Do not feel it's selfish as if their child has done all of the sacrificing, this is like the dance of the tango. It is a beautiful, melodic dance between souls moving together towards their crescendo of being their full enlightenment.

As you mother or father your child, you may feel that it is one sided, you are doing so much daily grind work. Now you learn this behind the scenes soul purpose stuff and feel like a pawn in a game of chess. But if you can see you working together at this higher level to move each other, then you can see a sort of symbiosis between you. Give, take, do this, do that, there is no score that can be judged when one is talking enlightenment. It is all relevant and irrelevant at the same time. It is all beautiful souls working together with no one getting short changed in the big picture perspective.

Do you know how loved and honored you are? Do you understand what a valuable role you play in humanity today? Because these children have such a heightened sensitivity, they have already taught humanity so much. Their teachings may not be accepted quite yet but there is a growing surge of power behind those lessons that is forcing the stubborn ones to listen. Who spoke of GMO's, toxic ingredients in food ten years ago? No one. But now, look at the momentum building so strongly that many are unsuccessfully able to deny. The mothers and fathers were an integral part in pushing this through because of the impact physically they saw with their children. So parents, you are the ambassadors for change and the children are the teachers to show you through their bodies what needs to be changed. See the dance? It's beautiful!

I speak to you as one of the chosen ones to help bring discovery to your awareness about your soul purpose. It's easy to allow yourself to be forgotten or become the martyr in your life and not really know what purpose you hold. Are you just the simple caregiver here that makes life as comfortable as possible for your child? I attest that you hold a more sacred role than that. You are the blessed mothers like Mary was to Jesus. She is held in high regard because as the story tells she "listened" to her calling and was steadfast in fulfilling her role. You are the Marys of the world and your child is the embodiment of Jesus. He brings messages and blessings and miracles to the world. You listen and hold the space and love for him to do that. It's a sacred blessing and a sacred calling.

Fathers hold a different role but just as holy. Fathers hold a grounding energy in the home. They are the providers, they are the engine that keeps this car running. Mothers sometimes get frustrated with their husbands, but that is because they truly don't understand their role in this journey. They have a whole other connection with their child than the mother and cannot be expected to have the same connection. Fathers are creating opportunities for work to get done. They are working hard in the three dimensional world to provide food, shelter and space for the family to evolve. Please understand that this role is much more grounded in reality but just as important as every other role here. It is not to be marginalized one bit.

Siblings also play an important role. Many hold very sacred gifts as well that may be ignored until it's time for them to shine. It may look like sacrifice or not getting enough in this world. I assure you these roles have been accepted with full knowledge before coming into this role. At the soul level, the siblings know that they are "supportive personnel" in this journey and gladly have accepted that position. Understanding this, we need not compare them to other children in different families, we only look at them within the context of our own family. We also have so much to learn from them, as siblings are teachers in their own right. Their lessons may be more subtle but just as powerful.

Can you see how the family dynamics here interplay and work together with a momentum of a Beethoven symphony? Even Beethoven created while deaf. You have created your life at times with deaf ears and blind eyes. This message and book serve as an uncovering of the blinders and a releasing of the muffled sound so you can now be clear here in all ways. As you read this, know that you are supported so much and feel the loving energy pouring from it for you because you deserve to access your full knowledge and full awareness of what your soul already knows. Be at peace. Be peace. Peace. That is who you are and what you bring to this world.

A Message from Eric

I enjoy my life immensely. It is one of great blessings and hard work. But I enjoy my life. On the surface yes, I cannot read, write or speak much, but I enjoy my life. Yes, inside my tummy may hurt, my muscles may ache, my head may pound, but I enjoy my life. Why would I enjoy my life even with these struggles? These struggles are not who I am or who I will be. They are a minor inconvenience at this time and really more troublesome to those around me than to me. I am not as concerned about my physical body balance as I am with my spiritual work. I enjoy my life and what I do and who I am.

Although Archangel Metatron is not a child diagnosed with autism, he is the Archangel who is Omni-present with our families and is working hand in hand with us. He is asking to bring a message at this place in the book for you to read.

A Message from Archangel Metatron

I wanted to write in this book to tell you of the role I play in your life. I was once in a human body and understand how it feels to be in the density of flesh and bones. I understand how it feels to not know where your next meal will come from and if you will take another breath. I understand. The reason these children and adults have come through so boldly at this time with such a hidden intelligence within is to shift the world. This may sound like a grandiose prospect, an unrealistic goal, but it is definitely what is happening. People will make gross estimates at the percentage of the population that will be diagnosed with autism in the near future. It sounds like fear mongering and it is to some extent. But the truth of the reality is that it is happening. It is happening whether one is vaccinated or not. If that child holds a soul purpose to be part of this evolution of the human species then they will hold that energy in some way.

Many current children came to realize their soul purpose due to an injury or intrusion of some sort. That cannot be denied. But one can never view them as victims if that injury propelled them into their soul purpose and essence of being. Know that it would have happened one way or the other. They would find their way regardless of the circumstances. Some hold the purpose to teach of vaccine and chemical dangers, so their teachings came through that experience. Others bring lessons about food, ingredients and pesticides so that is their path of teaching. It's one-way or the other. The DNA does play a crucial role as the new genetics were spawned out of damage to the environment and emotional trauma but this is the way it is. These susceptibilities they have were put into motion as ancestral blood DNA patterns many, many generations ago. The rumblings of the Earth made it known that the path being taken by humanity was destructive. A destructive path would likely result in destructive patterns merging generations down the line.

Yet the souls coming into these bodies knew, and took forth the challenge to embody those patterns, recognize them and forge through to turn back around and teach and heal the present and the past, lifting the ban on a future filled with deeper damage and patterns. Currently we are in a shifting pattern of awareness. It truly is a wonderful time to live! What part will you hold in this new evolution of human species? I assure you, it is a valuable role.

Chapter 9:
Mother's Awakenings

Here I share with you some beautiful stories shared from the hearts of mothers. What each has in common is an unconditional acceptance and love for their child as they got to know and understand their purpose with each other. My intention here is for you to read their words and relate to all or parts of their story and infuse that into your story with your child. What is your story?

Lucia and Alex

It all started Wednesday, November 1st, 2006, the time 10:05pm. My life as I knew it, would never be the same. With his birth, I was also born, the woman I was meant to be came to life that very cold winter night. I had no idea what was to come, another human being depended on me and without knowing it at that moment, it turned out I depended on him even more. He was so small, so fragile I thought, but at the same time, his presence was bigger than life itself. As I watched him lying there peacefully sleeping, I dreamed about all the things we would do together, all the adventures we would have. I remember even crying about the first day of school, as I just couldn't imagine being away from him. I thought to myself, how can this tiny little human mean so much to me already? I just met him. The love I felt for him was indescribable, it was stronger than anything I had ever felt before, how could it be?

The more I looked into his eyes, the more I fell in love, he captured my heart with every tiny movement, with every tiny touch. I asked myself if I was capable of taking on such a task, being this little boy's mother would change my life in every possible way. Was I ready for it? I had so many questions, yet somehow felt very safe being by his side. His presence gave me a confidence and security I never had before him. I was finally where I needed to be. I had another life that wanted to be in mine as much as I needed to be in his. He gave my life meaning, he was my reason for living. He was my son.

As the years went by, I realized he was special and not your ordinary everyday special, a kind of special that was so unique, so rare. I knew we had a strong connection, but before, I didn't know just how powerful it could be. I couldn't see it. It's not something you can see, it's something only felt in the heart. All this time I thought this connection was so I could save him. Little did I know the one that needed saving was me. He opened a whole new world to me, he saved me, and now I know everything we've been through was in a master plan, it was written.

Now that I know he communicates with me the best way he knows how, life makes a lot more sense. I recognize his signs, I hear his messages, I am being lead and following along is easier. See, he doesn't use spoken words to guide me, it's much bigger than that. Before, his silence was my prison, now I know it's my freedom. There are messages that aren't meant to be spoken or heard, they are meant to be felt in the heart. Those little messages I get from him many call "intuition." I just know them as my son talking to me. He's always talked to me, he's led me this far. He gave me the freedom I thought I would never have. He wants my happiness, my healing, I know that when I smile he smiles, he lives. Today, I know we are so connected that my pain is his, my joy is ours, my life and his are intertwined, we are one. I see through his eyes, he sees through my soul, it's always been this way, I now know. He has set me free, he knows where we're going, and I happily follow. Our journey is far from over, but knowing we are hand in hand makes it worthwhile.

Alex, you have taught me more in your lifetime than I ever learned in mine.

Melanie and Siana

Five years ago, the most perfect baby girl Siana entered my life. She was perfect. However, from the start I knew something was different about her. She had the biggest, bluest eyes you had ever seen, and everywhere we went she was like a magnet, everyone stopping us to see her. She met all her developmental milestones very early and was a very easy baby. Around the age of 18 months, her differences started to become obvious, she entertained herself happily for hours and was in her own little happy world. However, we didn't take much notice as she was verbal, extremely intelligent and she could recognize all of the letters and numbers by 18 months old and recite over 20 nursery rhymes word for word (I didn't realize how amazing this was until I had two other children). As Siana grew older, she started to have some hypersensitive sensory issues, she reacted badly to any food sources that were artificial and she was not interested in interacting with others except for her imaginary friends (I'm guessing they were a lot safer for her). She was very affectionate with people, but not at all interested in playing or talking to anyone. Siana could read places and people very well, any negative energy anywhere and she told us about it, mainly through crying. She loved animals though and was absolutely brilliant in all ways when she was in nature. She had no problem interacting with animals and trees.

Siana had many imaginary friends and talked about many different places. From early on, she never really asked for anything, but I always knew what she wanted. One day we were out walking with my other two children and I was having conversations in my head (I didn't realize I was doing so) and Siana turned around to me and said "Who are you talking to?" That is when I realized she was telepathic and that I was living way too much in my head. I had thought throughout my life that I may have been telepathic, but had doubted it, and on that day, she awakened me to the reality of telepathic communication.

She also made me become aware that I lived in my head and was mostly unconscious of what was going on in most of my present moments.

One year after this incident, when Siana was five years old, we started having many problems with her having no conscious awareness and she continually was living in her head, we only knew this because she verbalized it all, she spoke out loud everything she was thinking. One day, I was sitting there and contemplating why she would be doing this (no therapists or teachers knew either) and I had a big aha moment. She was doing exactly what I was doing, although she was speaking it aloud, it was that moment I knew I had to change and had to start living in the present moment, in the now, and move out of my head. From that moment I started living in the present moment, and so did she. She was mirroring me and likely many adults around her, but out loud.

She awakened me to the reality of telepathy and the beautiful art of conscious awareness. I have made so many shifts and learned so much about myself and life since she came into my life. She is a challenge to parent, but my goodness she has changed my life in ways I could not have imagined, all for the better.

My son, my teacher: Chari and Richard

From the moment I started paying attention to my pregnancy with Richard, I knew he would be special. I didn't realize just *how* special he would be. His kind of special would put me on a life altering journey which to date I have not completed. During my pregnancy, I would dream of water. Whether it was the beach, a pool, a lake, fish in a bowl, there was always lots of water. Then there was the very specific dream about two indigo blue fish in a fish bowl. That dream would stay with me forever.

Indeed, Richard was born a Pisces on a cold February evening. The fun began shortly after the anesthesia of my C-section started wearing off. It was the first time both of us would be awake enough to finally look into each other's eyes. I was rocking him in my new glider. As I looked into the big brown eyes of my newborn, I had a strange feeling of familiarity. "Who are you?" I thought. Then, like an answer to my unspoken question I hear, "Oh, it's so good to finally see you again." What? Who said that? I looked around. No one else was there, yet I was hearing these words in my head. I looked at his eyes again and the words kept flowing into my head. It went something like, "I've waited so long to see you again. We have a lot to do together." Not being as enlightened as I am now, I freaked out. My conscious thought was, "Oh my God! I've given birth to a Martian!"

At about three years old, and not yet diagnosed, Richard had some speech. Every now and then, seemingly out of nowhere he would run around saying single words as if he were saying a mantra. For example, he once said "gratitude" over and over again to me. This was from a toddler who had a speech delay. The kicker came when I let him run around our busy law office where he got to observe the distressed legal assistants on the phone with clients. He would say "Patience, patience, patience" right on cue. Richard would become my oracle. Yet it would be years before I fully understood that he was my teacher and I followed his lead.

When he was around six or seven years old, I was home-schooling him. I ran a Son-Rise program where I needed to keep half a dozen volunteers motivated to keep coming back to my apartment and try to engage my little one for hours at a time. I had won a free ticket to a Tony Robbins "Unleash the Power Within" motivational weekend seminar. I figured I'd learn some motivational skills from the best. I went by myself and sat with people I didn't know. It seemed that emotions swung from introspection to elation depending upon what Robbins was speaking about or the music they played. The energy of 4,000 people permeated the convention center and was palpable.

I had many powerful experiences that weekend. At the end of the first night, Robbins guided and expected as many people as possible to walk over hot coals. Even with all the preparation hours before, I did not think I had the guts to do this. Yet, walk over 1,200 degree Fahrenheit coals I did, with the encouragement of an "angel" that came out of nowhere and led me outside.

As I stepped off the coals, I heard Richard's voice as clear as day. He said, "I will find my voice when you find yours." He would go on to utter prophetic words and phrases as he grew older. I knew his mission here on Earth was not only to help me, but as many others as he could. It's been at least ten years since then, and I think I've finally found my voice. Almost on cue, Richard's speech has blossomed into full sentences at the ripe old age of seventeen.

We have an uncommon bond. If I would get sick, a few hours later he would also, without me having gone near him. Our bond would be confirmed when we started working with Tami. I would have to learn to keep my thoughts as positive as possible. There is still a lot of work that we both must do, however there is no doubt that as I heal, so does he.

Laura and Trevor

I was raised in the Catholic religion, so I had always believed in life after death in theory. However, I truly began to become awakened to the divine essence of all of us after losing my first spouse twenty years ago and began communicating with him through mediums. I was given undeniable proof that we exist after our body no longer lives. I also received messages from my grandparents and friends in the spirit world, and even talked to my dad on the day he crossed over through a medium.

After my son Trevor was born (diagnosed at age three with regressive autism), I began receiving messages from those in spirit about how I could help my son heal during my sessions with mediums. Later on, I teamed up with a medium and a spirit artist couple, and actually wrote a channeled book called "The Other Side of Autism." I was told about the causes and remedies to help children with regressive autism. I took the advice of those in spirit and my son improved.

In an effort to heal my son, I investigated alternative modalities, and had a Reiki session with someone at a psychic fair, and felt some powerful things happening in my body. I knew I had to learn how to do this to help my child. I became a Reiki Master, then a few years later, learned how to do Reconnective Healing, another form of energy healing. I can't tell you how many times I've used this to help calm, comfort, and heal not just my son, but my whole family, friends, and even strangers. I also energetically charge my son's bathwater and drinking water, and do distance healing on him from the other room or while he is at school.

I had a phone session with Tami last year, and she blew me away. She told me things about my son that she couldn't possibly have known otherwise. It was more proof that our kids are telepathic, and understand everything that is going on around them, even if they can't verbally communicate fully. It is one thing to talk to dead people, but another thing entirely to have a medium tell you what your living verbally challenged child is saying. The process is similar, it is a telepathic form of communication. I aim to learn this myself soon, but for now, I have my intuition, and resources like Tami when I need more answers. She is such a gift to our kids, not to mention the moms.

In addition to Tami, I have had other sessions with very gifted mediums and trance channels, and through these communications, I have come to believe that our kids chose this path, as we did, before we came into this physical body. There is a much bigger reason than we know as to why, but it is serving the collective consciousness. I know this flies in the face of logic of an angry autism parent, but there truly is more going on than meets the eye. Once you learn about our true spiritual nature, and let go of the religious dogma most of us were raised in, you start to see life in a whole new way. You start to see your child with new eyes. When you begin to see their true essence, and how brave they were for choosing this role, you see that they are true heroes. They are here to change the world, and they will.

Chapter 10:
Father's Awakenings

Keith and Christian

My name is Keith McClelland, my wife's name is Mallory and together we have two beautiful children. Christian is four and Callie is three. Mal is also the stepmother to my three children from my previous marriage Keith Jr. (13), Myles (11) and Keira (10). Our journey began before Christian was even born. Mallory read a lot of articles during her pregnancy about vaccines and their link to autism. I had completely dismissed the notion and explained that it was just a myth, and that there was nothing wrong with my three older children who were all fully vaxxed. The conversation didn't come up again until Christian was ready for his first round of shots, where she again asked me if I was sure this was the right decision for our son's health. Looking back now, I realize how incredibly closed minded I was.

I should preface that by saying I was born in 1971. That's relevant because I'm part of generation that had been spoon-fed our information, before things really took a turn for the worse. Yes, they vaccinated in the 70's but it's nothing like the vaccines that kids are receiving now. I drank milk regularly and always believed it was good for me. GMO's had not yet been introduced into our food system. Autism was a word most people never heard of, etc. That was the foundation of beliefs I carried with me until my wife and I started having our disagreements. At that point, I was like everyone else who was brainwashed with disinformation and chose to believe what the doctors and media were telling us was true. They were the experts, they were the ones who had PhD's. My wife chose to trust me over her gut instinct and we went ahead with his first of many rounds of shots. Back and forth the debate went over the next couple years, as Mallory started to investigate the "myths" as I had put it and come to a new understanding of vaccinations and modern medicine, while I continued to dismiss her opinion and categorize her as a beginner parent who didn't know what she was talking about, and a kook.

For the first year of life, Christian received vaccines on a delayed schedule. He was developing normally with some eczema and ear infections sprinkled in. By the time Christian was a year old, Mal and I shared very different opinions about where he should be developmentally. Mallory was convinced something was wrong with Christian, and was not developmentally where he should be. I argued that he was perfectly normal and healthy, and all kids progress on their own schedule. I can remember it so clearly when I told my wife that "she was not a doctor," and "she doesn't know what she was talking about." I also remember telling her so many times that "Christian will talk when he is ready." Much to the credit of my wife, she chose to follow her gut and disregard what her husband, relatives, close friends, doctors, and mainstream media were telling her. Through all of that, Mallory continued to do her research and then email me stories and articles that supported her position on an almost daily basis. This was a tense time in our marriage as we were on completely opposite ends in our beliefs, but then something incredible happened. I slowly began to entertain the notion that she might be right.

I began to look at our son with an open mind and started looking for the evidence of what she was talking about all along. I allowed myself to unwind all of the spoon-fed statistics which I was brainwashed to believe and when that happened, I saw Christian as well as the world with a whole new clarity. Within a day or so of my awakening, there were major alarms going off in my head as to the development of Christian and for the first time, I could clearly see what Mal had been talking about all along. It was shortly after that that Christian was diagnosed with apraxia, and was on the autism spectrum. Because we had caught it so early, it gave us an opportunity to heal him much sooner and quicker. I am so grateful that Mallory did not give up on me and I'm grateful that a subconscious part of me allowed the info to seep in so that I could open my mind and be awakened. To this day, I'm not sure that our marriage would've survived without my transformation. In fact, after having attended many conferences and seminars with Mallory on the subject, I have observed that my awakening is in the minority, and a large number of marriages and families have been destroyed over this subject matter. My heart pours out to those families, as it is no longer hard for me to feel their pain and suffering, and I find myself wanting to help them in any way I can. Perhaps telling our story will open the door for other closed minded dads to open their minds, and allow the possibility of the truth to enter in.

Now, it may seem like my awakening was the end of the journey, but really it was only the beginning. Mallory and I were now a team, and shared the exact same goal of healing our son by whatever means necessary. Mallory had connected to various autism groups, and it wasn't long before our knowledge and understanding of how the medical industry really works in the world, was expanding exponentially. We had shifted our pursuit to healing our son from modern medicine, to holistic, homeopathic, and spiritual healing. Through her networking, Mallory had become close with some local moms who were part of a group called the *Thinking Moms' Revolution*. I can't stress how instrumental these women were with helping put us on the right path to lead to Christian's recovery.

There was a woman in that group named Sadie who mentored us and continues to mentor us throughout it all, even while she has a son who also has ASD and Apraxia. One day, Sadie was talking to Mallory about Tami Duncan, and how Tami has been able to make huge breakthroughs with her son in a way that some would not believe is possible. She was able to communicate with his light, which can also be considered his spirit, his ego, or his inner self. Mallory was very excited to discuss this with me in hopes that I would be in agreement that we give her a try. Strangely enough, this was not a hard leap of faith for me at all despite my previously discussed close-mindedness. In fact, it was a much easier leap for me than Mallory. There were some events that I was directly involved in during my youth through today which had allowed me to easily accept Tami's abilities, as well as her methods of healing. So after discussing it, Mallory and I decided to give Tami a try.

The session with Christian turned out to be beyond a "wow" moment. She had touched on topics that we kept very tight to the chest, and were only really known by Mallory and myself. More than that though, she was able to connect with our son and give us great insight on what we can do to further his recovery. We implemented her recommendations immediately, and the improved results were almost instantaneous! To this day, we continue to have sessions with Tami and not just Christian. I have had multiple sessions with Tami, as well as Mallory and all five of my kids.

The journey for us continues to be a daily one, as our knowledge continues to grow. Christian is now four, and continues to improve, but he still has more healing to do. We were told just last week from his therapists that he will be attending kindergarten in a neurotypical class-room, which is what our goal was. He will continue to get some of his therapies while in school, but were are so proud of him and what a long way he has come. To the moms who struggle to find a way to get their husbands or their child's father to understand what is happening, I hope our story finds you and gives you the courage to continue to get the message across. I can't guarantee that they will experience the same level of awakening that I did, but I am certain that eventually on some level, they will hear you and then I pray that together, you too can heal your child.

The Wonderful World of Zander

My name is Corey. My son Zander was brought into the world like most normal children. He had a typical modern day upbringing throughout his infant/toddler time. He had ear infections, consistent head colds, fevers, and other medical issues. We never questioned the doctors because they were the experts. If he was sick we would just give him more OTC or Rx medication as needed. His diet was not very healthy. He was fully vaccinated to schedule up to his reaction-injury.

His speech and normal progression was a tick slower, but he spoke and played and had a huge smile. After the MMR vaccine he regressed quite a bit, but we didn't see the full signs. Our daughter was up for a round of shots and she was given the Chicken pox shot. We were asked if we wanted to give it to Zander as well. This was the straw that broke the camel's back. He lost everything. No speech, no visual contact, no physical interaction. We had to force him to go to sleep. My wife Lori knew something was wrong, but I discounted it, saying that it was a part of growing up. But it continued to get worse. Lori told me after five to six months of watching it get ugly (self-mutilating and non-responsive to own name) that she thought he was autistic. I hadn't heard that before, and thought no way did we have an autistic child.

After she googled "recover autism" that's when the work started. On all these Google searches came three that always stood out. Generation Rescue, GF/CF diet, and DAN! doctors. So that's what we did. We threw away all the food in the house and replaced it with GF/CF foods. After eating what seemed at the time gross powdered foods for two days, Zander responded to his name for the first time in over a year. And then again when I called out for him a week later. That was the moment I was fully on board with this alternative recovery ship!

We went to Seattle to see a DAN! doctor twice. The first time was to spill our guts to her. We left having to get a bunch of labs done and had an appointment a month later. During our wait, the research went on and on. Upon our return, we had a boatload of questions and requests. The doctor didn't like our eagerness to get our recovery process going. She took it as we were challenging her medical authority. Which 30 minutes into the appointment she looked at us and said "Here, you want to be the doctor?" We promptly walked out and continued our search.

Enter Drs. Amy Derksen and Elizabeth Sheehan. We heard through a friend about Dr. Amy and made an appointment to see her. Blown away is the best was to sum up our visit. We had never heard of muscle testing before. Through muscle testing, she found that he had a lot of trapped viruses and some heavy metals. We started to work on these issues through chelation and other supplements. After a couple visits she recommended that we see Dr. E., as we call her now. She is a Naturopathic Chiropractor that does Quantum Neurology. She was the one responsible for getting his speech back together. She also does a lot of different testing processes which found other underlying issues within Zander that took years of work. Recovering children from autism is a marathon and is similar to the onion theory. Peel and peel to discover new issues that were not present before.

In between all of these visits we were also seeing a Chinese herbalist for Eastern Medicine and Acupuncture treatment for Zander. He introduced us to a product called LDM100. After a few weeks of taking this Zander had two days of excreting the Measles and Rubella viruses all over his body. A day later was the first time he ever drew anything. He drew a smiley face. What a break out this was to see. The other doctors were amazed with the improvements.

We found that after the onion effect, we constantly had issues with candida overgrowth. It was difficult to stay on top of this but after rounds of supplements and even one Rx (Nystatin) to kill of the yeast, we finally had it under control.

Through all of this, we lost everything. My business, house, cars, savings, everything was used to heal Zander. Filing bankruptcy was a difficult, trying time. Through the smoke we found solace within the situation. We chose to start over and moved to Talent, Oregon (right outside of Ashland) with minimal reserves. We found a great home, and an even better community. I located a good job and started flourishing. The family and I really enjoyed our time there and were able to detox from the city life. Ashland has such a great vibe and granola lifestyle. Zander enjoyed southern Oregon life.

I was offered a promotion and we moved to the NW suburbs of Chicago. Life was rough there. Not only the brutal weather but the food situation is nearly impossible. Being that we live a mostly organic lifestyle, shopping was a challenge. There are Whole Foods and Costco stores, and that's about it. Not a great place for healthy living. We learned a lot and had an experience to share in the future. We needed to get out of that place because no one was happy living there.

So off to Portland, Oregon we went. We lived in Vancouver, WA and started really enjoying life again. Zander was in a happy place. We were close to all of our doctors again, so that was nice. About two months after moving into our house, we were all involved in an auto accident. Zander was really traumatized from it, like he was stuck in that event. Lori jumped on Facebook and asked what we should do to help us out. We had not established any local help or services. Dr. E. told us to use our doTERRA essential oils. Once we had a protocol with Zander, we started treating him. Instantly he let go of the attachment of the accident. Our recovery from the physical side (pain) was faster with the oil usage.

We stayed there for about a year before taking off to head back to the U.P. area in Washington. We chose to move to be closer to our family and doctors. It gave us a different dimension to return back to the U.P. because our mindset on life is so different. We have been able to find and have closure from the past of everything we went through.

Now Zander is 11, and he's about as neurotypical as you could ask for. He loves Minecraft, reading books, filming mini videos, making animation videos, and having multiple blogs. He loves to play with his younger brother Zeppelin (4) and helping him learn.

From Tami: To me, I find the perspective of the fathers absolutely fascinating. Really, they are bringing in what they saw from their viewpoint. As a mother we expect our husbands to see things the same way we do, to have the same "aha" moments that we do. But that isn't realistic because we each have a different connection to our children. Zander's mom was surprised to see her husband's perspective much different from hers. As we discussed, we realized that his perspective was perfect because it was his journey with Zander.

I asked my husband about his journey with Michael and his report was very much similar to Corey's. He works very hard, and as much as I thought he was living it with me, he was seeing it from the outside and from a more grounded place. Men just think differently than women. My husband may see cause and effect, black and white, where I see all the grey, the intricacies in between the results.

Isn't it fascinating? My lesson is that it's OK. He doesn't need to see it "my way" and he shouldn't because he hasn't experienced Michael in the same way I have.

Lori's perspective on Zander's story

Zander's recovery started when we began healing the whole family. Although I thought it was about the bio-medical work we had done, I began to realize that his true recovery began later. When we began to accept him for who he is instead of who we thought he should be, that is when he truly improved.

Moving away from the area that held so much of the association with illness was key for us. The house, the location all represented illness and autism. We needed to find our family healing area. A mother wants to fix her child, but when I learned that he wanted to be accepted and didn't want to be labeled because it was his crutch or illness, I was able to let everything go and turned it over to him. He decided where to go. He could choose. He chooses not to be associated with autism except in that it is something he went through in his childhood. He is free of it.

Another part for me was stepping away from the autism warrior mama energy out there. It was very healing. It was more crippling to me to be involved with the negativity and needed to release from that. There is a lot of fear energy put out there if you don't do certain treatments that your child may never get better. I stopped believing any of those stories and let go of those connections.

I began finding out each family member's journey was individual for themselves. They found their own healing path and we began working together. Zander improved in such ways we could never get with biomedical treatment. His creativity really blossomed.

I really noticed that he had some kind of gifts because he kept seeing things in mirrors. It was irritating to him, and he was able to be comfortable without the mirrors. I didn't question him, I understood and believed him that he was seeing things. In this way, I allowed him to trust that I honored his emotions about things.

Zander talks about God and we are not a religious family. He talks about heaven, he says that God doesn't like when people lie. That's not the way they do things in heaven, he says. He has his own way of thinking. When he is truthful to his thoughts, he tells us what it is. We allow him to express himself in his trueness.

Our awakening is for all of us. Accepting what is. Dr. Elizabeth Sheehan was huge for our awakening as well, both with physical as well as energetic understanding. She taught us that the answer is right in front of you. It is important to have a supportive practitioner on board who understands not only the physical, but the emotional, mental and spiritual aspects of healing as well. We all are part of this awakening. Our family is a unit, has its own energy and understanding. Zander opened us all to understanding more about ourselves.

Chapter 11:
Energetic Techniques for Daily Life

The concepts in this book may be new to you, or you may have heard of some of them if you study metaphysics. But really, we are talking about energy and how energy can influence us, both our energy and others, and how that also affects our child. Let's talk about some things that you can start incorporating into your daily life to help shift the energy into a positive, light-filled vibration.

Holding Space

As parents, we are programmed to guide and correct behaviors. But what if that behavior was an expression of an emotion or something that needed to come out of the body? It's not bad behavior, it's more of an episode. As adults, we have these episodes all that time, it's just that we don't have our parents in our face correcting us all the time. This is where the holding space concept comes in.

Let's say that your child is having a meltdown. It looks on the surface like a tantrum because it had to do with taking the iPad away. But under the surface it could be something else at play. Does that iPad provide him comfort, relaxation, a way to block out sensory input that is disturbing to him? By taking it away, did that cause him stress because it took away his "crutch" that was helping him keep more balanced? Understanding the underlying cause here is key to deciding how you should respond.

In this situation you could choose to stand your ground and let him be mad and continue to keep it from him. You could give it back to shut him up. Or you could drop into your heart and work to understand him and why he is reacting in this way. When you drop into your heart truly, you can find that answer. Holding space is a strategy you can possibly use.

Holding space is simply keeping a neutral balance in yourself while he is expressing his emotions. You are supporting and loving him and completely keeping your cool no matter what he is doing. Sounds simple right? Sometimes yes, but in aggressive situations, not so easy. In aggressive situations it is even more important that you hold firm to your neutrality. This means you don't allow your temper, fear, sadness or anxiety to be seen at all during the episode. You remain cool and detached, yet loving. You aren't coddling, trying to hug or comfort either. You are stable and really neutral. This may mean that the episode goes a little longer than usual because you aren't "taking the bait" and reacting. That's ok though, because you are holding space, you are holding the vibration in the room that can allow him to come back into balance....and hopefully sooner than usual. If you allow your emotions to intertwine with his, then you are in for a train wreck and an escalation of emotions that can be hard to come back from. It's kind of like not allowing your buttons to be pushed. We all know kids love to do this regardless of an autism diagnosis. The better we can hold that space the less they try it.

Shifting the Energy

What you have done here really is shifted the energy. You have taken one vibration of let's say anger, which is a lower vibrating emotion, and by remaining neutral you have made space for him to come to neutral as well.

You can shift the energy in many ways and in many situations. Just know that you have the power to decide what energy you put out into the world. If you are bringing a lot of anger, sadness, resentment and fear into your home, then you are likely to get that back from others. As humans we tend to match each other's energy inadvertently. When you are aware of this, then you can shift it. The key here it to catch yourself and ask "Am I putting love into the world through my thoughts, words and actions?" If the answer is no, then begin to broaden your awareness on this topic.

An example here would be to work on bringing high vibrational energy into the home. These are emotions like:

> Love
> Joy
> Compassion
> Peace
> Playfulness
> Gratitude

These are such beautiful vibrations that when you put them into the world, it is contagious! These high vibrations are exactly what the children are calling from us. In some cases the children are DEMANDING this unconditional love vibration from our hearts. When we realize that we can be in our own power and choose, then we have made a big step in holding a high vibrational space which allows even more room for these emotions to come from your child as well. In essence, it really is the best way to live and to teach by example of how to live our lives.

I realize it's not always easy to "be" these positive vibrations all the time. Even just a little bit of effort in this direction will make a difference. We will talk a little later about strategies you can utilize to infuse these energies into your life and your home.

Affirmations

Creating affirmations is a very important tool for creating and manifesting positivity into your life. Although it may be very tempting for you to create intentions and affirmations for your child, it is best to start with yourself. I say this because we always need to consider the free will of all. If you are creating intentions for your child, on their behalf, are you certain that this is what they want? Are you certain it is in their highest good? You may be infringing your own desires on them. So start with yourself. This is your step in raising your vibration to a higher, more loving level. As I've said before, when you work on yourself, it allows space for others to move and evolve as well, in their time and it being their choice.

Know that the first thing is to decide what you would like to accomplish. I recommend starting with very general concepts. For me, it was all about peace and balance. I wanted to create more balance in my life as it felt off. I was spending too much time working and not enough time playing. There is a balance that can be achieved. I also felt out of balance with my personality. I was both super loving and understanding or locked up and tense, bordering on the edge of angry. This out of balance thing was a big deal for me. I spent several New Year's Resolutions on this without much success until I changed my inner thought patterns. Inside, I was thinking about how out of balance I was. So I was feeding the pattern by thinking about it. This is negative manifesting. If you think you are sick, you are. If you think you are out of balance, you are. So how do we break that pattern? Reverse it! A good start is to reverse it with affirmations.

Start by creating a list of intentions. It can be just one thing or 20 things. I would start off small though until you get the hang of it. In my example, my intentions were:

To create balance of work time, family time and emotions. To be peaceful in all aspects of my life.

Remember though that your intentions are only about YOU doing something, not someone else doing something. So it can't be "To get my son healthy." That would be infringing upon his journey. You can intend something more like this "To be open to receiving information for our healing journey." This way you can be lead to information instead of already deciding it is in his best interest to be healthy. The truth is that some people do come in this world to battle physical illness because there is much to learn from this. Unless you know for sure your child does not fit in this category, then work on just being open to being guided to the answers.

Now that we have set our intentions. It's time to begin manifesting them into our daily lives. Affirmations help to imprint whatever concept you are trying to do into your subconscious. I have found that it is very effective to begin my affirmations with the two words "I am." I AM represents your infinite self, your God self, your God within. What follows those two words, I AM, should represent the beauty and divinity of who you are. They are both empowering words and speak of the "light" within you. As you speak of your light you speak of God's light. It's one and the same. This concept is really beautifully taught in Wayne Dyer's book, _Wishes Fulfilled_, which I highly recommend.

Suggestions in creating your affirmations

1. Take your intention we set in the last exercise and create a sentence from it. For example...my intention is to speak telepathically to my son. Or...my intention is to clear out any fear I have blocking me from connecting with my son, etc.

2. Now, reword that intention in the positive. (Take out any negative connotations.) For example...I speak telepathically to my son. Or...I am confidently connecting with my son.

3. If still needed, reword and add the two words I AM to the beginning. I AM speaking telepathically to my son. I AM confidently connecting with my son.

4. Make as many affirmations as you like. Whatever is coming to you even if it wasn't one of your original intentions, write it down. Create an affirmation. It can be one or twenty!

Now that you have your list of affirmations, let's put them into practice. Here are some ideas for imprinting these affirmations into your subconscious by using them in your daily life. Choose one or two from this list and do them each day.

1. Write each affirmation on a post-it-note or paper and post around your office, your bedroom, your bathroom. Put them in your visual field so you are seeing them multiple times during the day. You can also put them in your pocket and carry them with you during the day.

2. Chant them out loud or in your mind (or both) several times per day. If the mind pops in and says "That's not true!" ask your mind to step aside and allow your intuitive mind to come forward.

3. **Tape an affirmation to the side of a glass of water or water bottle.** Set the glass in the sun for 30 minutes to an hour. The water will be charged with the energy of the affirmation and it will imprint into your water. As you drink the water you will be charging your cells with the energy of the affirmation.

4. **Spend time in quiet reflection each day.** Imagine your affirmations, your intentions as a reality. Feel what it feels like for that to be true. Affirm that it is true by saying your affirmations quietly several times. Give thanks and gratitude that it IS true and it IS a reality.

5. **If you have done any kind of energy work before, like Reiki, imagine your affirmations as energy.** Hold that energy in your awareness. Give it a shape or a color. Infuse your solar plexus (right above your belly button) with the energy of your affirmations. Feel the energy of the affirmations infusing into your entire being.

6. **As you go to sleep at night ask yourself, "How does my body feel having all of my affirmations true to-night?"**

7. **Use your creativity and imagination to practice your affirmations.** Any idea that pops in will work, as that comes from your intuition, which is aligned to a higher source.

8. **Using EFT (Emotional Freedom Technique) to TAP your affirmations in.** Here is a link where you can find the tapping points. Simply just tap and chant your affir-

mation three times in each location. (Please ignore the verbiage they use on the website as that is not for this purpose.) http://eft.mercola.com/

What's important is feeling totally aligned with your affirmations. You may not in the beginning, but if after a few weeks of doing this you seem to be fighting with one of them, you are either not aligned with the concept or the wording, or you are blocking this one in some way. You would need to go in deep and ask yourself why you would be blocking this from your life. Is it fear, anxiety, worry, or do you feel unworthy of this kind of goodness? In any event, find the reason and then work to resolve it.

If your child is verbal, then you certainly can use the method above with them and they can participate in creating their own affirmations. Just don't lead them with your own agenda, allow them to speak freely and list their own intentions and then you can help guide them into affirmations. As you model this in your home, they will feel more able to be successful with these for themselves.

Setting the Space

The energy in the home and school environment is very important for a child diagnosed with autism. Many times, the environment isn't optimal because there is a lot of stress and fear energy. As parents, we are between two worlds. We are trying to race the clock for recovery by kindergarten, middle school, high school or adulthood.

We are also trying hard not to, but comparing our lives to other families. This combined with the daily grind of parenting, making special food, and trying to do everything "right" is very demanding. So it's no wonder there is a lot of stress energy. It's totally understandable. Yet, we can't let it control or dictate us. We need to step into our power to create balance in the home. Not everything is as important as it seems. We live in such fear of regression that when there are good times, we taint them with the fear that it might be taken away. With taking some extra time to create the space energy, your home will become the beautiful safe haven it is meant to be and transmute that stress energy to a thing of the past.

Here are some things to try. It really is an exhaustive list, so allow yourself to be open to other ideas that pop in as well.

Idea #1: Smudging an area

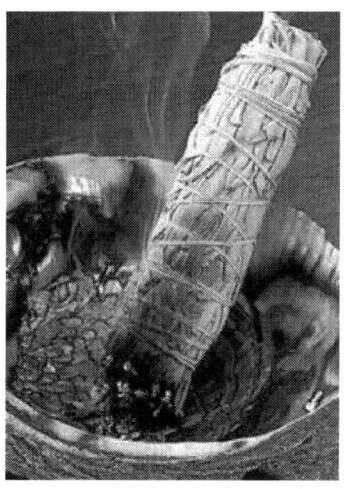

We talked about smudging earlier, but here is a more detailed description of what that is. Smudging is the common name given to the sacred smoke bowl blessing. It is a powerful cleansing technique from the Native North American tradition. Smudging calls on the spirits of sacred plants to drive away negative energies and restore balance. It is the art of cleansing yourself and your environment using simple ritual and ceremony. For thousands of years, smudging has been a part of Native American tradition but now its power of cleansing is available to everyone. Here's how:

1. Get a sage smudge stick, abalone shell and feather.

2. Light the smudge stick using a candle and blow the embers so that it produces smoke.

3. Start at your feet, and brush the smoke over the bottoms of your feet, working up the body to the crown. Use the intention that all negative energy will be cleared and removed from you and the space.

4. Do the same thing room by room beginning at the farthest corner from the front door. Move clockwise brushing the smoke to the corners of each room. Don't forget closets and bathrooms! Some choose to chant the Lord's Prayer or other positive phrases during this time.

5. Keep the front door open so that the negative energy can leave from the home.

Idea # 2: Essential Oils

As I mentioned in an earlier chapter, some people have found success with a combination of essential oils. You may consider this option, as many people are sensitive to the smoke or they may have allergies to it. Other oils can be diffused in a room for certain purposes. For example, I like to diffuse sweet orange oil when we need to put a little "happiness" in the space. You may also diffuse frankincense if you would like to create a "sacred space." I recommend learning muscle testing to determine the correct oils for your family. What oil is healing for one, could be harmful for another. I have noticed that my dogs are extremely sensitive to the oils, often causing my Pug to have high anxiety when I am not mindful of him when choosing the oil. With muscle testing, one can determine the oils that would be healing for all and not cause any negative effects. See the resource section in the back for muscle testing workshop information.

Idea #3: Gridding the Space

In certain rooms of my home, such as my healing room or bedroom, I like to create that room as a sacred space. This is a good thought if you would like to do this for your child's room or a very special room that you use for meditation, prayer, yoga or your spiritual practices. The method of gridding that I use is based on very basic principles of Sacred Geometry. Sacred Geometry is defined as:

"Sacred Geometry is the blueprint of Creation and the genesis of all form. It is an ancient science that explores and explains the energy patterns that create and unify all things and reveals the precise way that the energy of Creation organizes itself. On every scale, every natural pattern of growth or movement conforms inevitably to one or more geometric shapes. As you enter the world of Sacred Geometry you begin to see as never before the wonderfully patterned beauty of Creation."

As I'm smudging the room, I am tracing any openings in the room. As I walk clockwise around the room I "seal" any opening such as windows and doors or openings as I smudge. I trace the shape of the opening in this order.

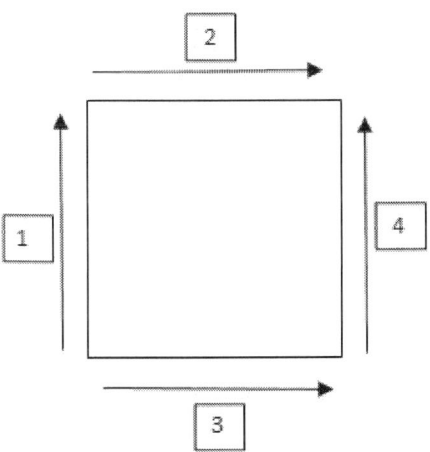

After tracing the walls, I then do the same process for the ceiling and the floor, so each surface has been smudged and traced in this fashion. From this point, you can add in Reiki symbols if you are a Reiki 2 or higher practitioner, or you may insert any sacred geometry symbols you would like to add. The purpose is to amplify the positive energy in the room. If your intention is for this room to be a protected, safe space then you can set that intention. If you would also like this room to emanate a sense of peace and calming, then set that intention. Whatever your intention IS, that will be done. As you are doing this process, you can talk to your guides, angels, and masters and ask for them assistance, support or confirmation. Your intention is powerful enough to create this.

When I mention sacred geometry symbols I am speaking of the flat shape of the below 3D shapes...

You would just draw one side and intend for the 3D shape to take form as it will. These shapes are known as the Platonic Solids and are known in every creation in the world, they are part of everything. Imagine the 3D shape taking form as you trace it in the air. With that shape comes the power of the Universe...the power of All that IS. There is no special method or reasoning for one or the other. Just do what you feel drawn to, what you feel guided to do.

Another way to use this method is the gridding and intention setting of the front and back door of your home. If you have people/family who enter into your home and bring their negative gunk in with them, a sensitive child will pick up on this. You may want to do a gridding on the doors they enter and set a strong intention that as they walk through, the grid will filter out and cleanse out any negative energy not in the highest good for all in the home. Imagine it like a fine mesh net that will gather up any muck and gunk. Empower the grid each day to strengthen and stay active. See any gunk gathered up transformed and sent to the light.

You may also grid the massage table, the sleeping bed or even the table for homework. The energy in those areas

will be infused with positive energy. You will have <
ed a sacred space for beautiful work to be done.

Idea # 4: Using Sound Frequencies

Certain sounds can clear and balance energy in the room.
There are many ways to do this.

- Ocean Drum by Remo – this is a wonderful drum
  that sounds like the ocean tide flowing in and
  flowing out. All you need to do is walk around the
  room with the intention that the sound frequency
  from the drum will cleanse the energy in the space.
  It is a vibration that cleanses.

- Gathering Drum by Remo – this is used in the
  same way as the ocean drum yet you are actively
  drumming with a mallet. Go through the space,
  drumming at whatever tempo you are guided to
  do. As you walk through, the speed may increase
  and even feel frantic, eventually it will slow as that
  energy is neutralized. Just continue to drum until
  you feel a nice and steady, relaxing beat.

- Sound healing music. I enjoy putting on music
  through the day to bring in certain frequencies into
  the home. When I am working and need to be
  deeply meditative, I play one thing, but when there
  is a lot of action and excitement I play something
  else. Here are some of my favorites:

Stephen Halpern – Chakra Suite - Great for overall balancing and can even be useful for lulling one to sleep.

Healing Music – Sleep Music for Relaxation – I find this a beautiful CD to play in the home when we want to just slow down any anxious energy. It can be found on iTunes.

Attuning to Oneness by Paradiso – This is my go-to album for meditation. I really love how it slowly moves your mind into silence. After a busy day and just needing peaceful rest of the mind, this one is wonderful.

Other- There are thousands of options out there. Specifically for clearing energy usually tracks with sound healing bowls, didgeridoo or tuning forks are effective.

Idea # 5: Calling in the Masters

Just by asking, it is done. You may begin to feel drawn to speaking with Masters such as Jesus, Blessed Mother Mary, Buddha, Quan Yin and others. You may also feel drawn to working with the Archangels. I have noticed that when we ask for help and are still in our own head or asking out of fear, it doesn't feel very powerful. This is because we are coming from a disempowered place. Yet when we take some time, some slow deep breaths, and ask for support with gratitude in our hearts, it is much ᵉᵃˢᶦer to feel this shift in energy. One can feel the support, the cleansing and even communicate more easily so you can receive messages from one of these highly evolved beings.

Idea # 6: Shift Your Energy

Through the simple act of changing your thoughts from negative to positive, you shift your energy. I have found a quick way to do this for myself is by using my mantra. It was mentioned in an earlier chapter by one of the boys. I want to share with you how this came to me.

In March 2014, I travelled to a small town in Brazil called Abadiania. This town is home of the trance medium known as John of God. I was on a healing retreat (which is a long story.) During the trip, I went into the room where hundreds of people meditate in silence in four hour shifts per day. I was concerned that I wouldn't be able to sit that long in the wooden church pews. My concern manifested when I got super wiggly and pondered faking the need to go to the bathroom. (Yeah, not my finest moment.) As I sat there trying not to bump the person next to me or jolt anyone else out of their meditative state, I asked, "What am I supposed to be meditating for?" Is this for ME or for THEM? By them, I mean the thousands of people walking through the room to receive their "healing" from John of God. At that moment, this mantra was given to me...

> I am love
> I am light
> I am joy
> I am peace
> As I heal
> Others heal
> As others heal
> I heal
> We are One
> In divine light

I repeated this over and over and over. I felt the wiggles and uncomfortableness leave my body. I no longer felt my body, except to feel complete love and peace in my heart. I was able to stay for the full four hours and came home with a beautiful mantra, a beautiful tool that I can now use to raise my vibration, stop my worrying mind, and allow the peace and love within me to shine through.

Possibly my mantra resonates with you, or possibly not. In any event, you may think of things that raises your vibration in this way. What makes your heart fill with love? By doing that thing, you raise your vibration, by raising your vibration you shift the energy in your home or any space you encounter. This will always be good for you and good for your child.

Another way I raise my vibration, which I realize sounds totally silly, is looking at cute puppy pictures and videos. Even the cats sometimes work too! It's no wonder watching animal videos is one of the most popular things to do on the internet. People thirst for happiness.

Shedding the Labels

Did you notice the title of the book says "AKA Awesome Kids?" This is because I choose not to label any child. A label in essence is an energetic curse. It is not intended to be evil or destructive in this sense, but a label becomes a way of identifying someone. Just like your name is your identification. Your label takes on that same power. It becomes static and to many it becomes "who they are."

So many families are striving for recovery. They want their child healthy, strong, active in the community and communicating. If we want that, then that is not what they say autism is. Autism is the opposite of that. If we say our child is autistic, it's like saying his name is Sam. How can Sam break free of that if it is his identity? In my presentations you will see me dance around the label and always say "a child diagnosed with autism" rather than a child having autism or being autistic. It's because I choose not to ever lock anyone into any identity or reality. We can certainly move through or flow through a diagnosis, then it becomes an experience and not a concrete thing. One can say their child exhibits autistic like symptoms and keep a flow that can allow the child to move in or move out of those symptoms.

It truly is about the law of attraction. Do you want recovery? Then to manifest that, we have to change our whole viewpoint, our thoughts and our vision of how we see our child. You will see what you want to see. If you look for behaviors, well you will get them. If you look for their spiritual essence, you will see that too.

This really hit home for me when my son Michael was in the 6th grade. He had a one-on-one aide who would help him pack his backpack, organize, stay on task, etc. One day as we sat to do nightly homework, I asked him where his folder for that day was. He said he didn't know. Then he went on to blame "Miss Kim," his aide, for not packing his backpack correctly. I said, "Well, why didn't you make sure you had everything?" He said, "That's her job, not mine!" At that moment, I knew he didn't need an aide any longer and had fallen into his label and became stagnant to accept what everyone thought of him. They didn't think he could do it, so he acted like the boss and delegated to his aide! Once we took away his crutch, it was amazing how much he found out he could do. Even at home with chores, I guess we just assumed he couldn't do it. Now he does all the stuff I don't like to do, and enjoys making money for it.

When I was healing from Lyme disease, I learned that it is very common in that community to refer to yourself as a "Lymie." One day, I realized that the "Lymie" label was locking me in a box of having that disease. So all at the same time, I declared publicly, "I no longer have Lyme disease." Then I told Michael, "You used to have autism because the doctors thought you did, but you don't anymore." Holy smokes! Michael made huge jumps in his skills and I healed my body of disease very quickly after that. Was I just falsifying the reality? One could think that but I prefer to think of it as strongly manifesting alignment with our soul purpose, which for me, I needed to go through illness to learn what it feels like so I can help others. And Michael's autism experience was something he needed to go through. It is all still being revealed to both of us, but none of it was a mistake, I know that for sure.

We shed the labels! When we believe with our whole hearts, we create that reality. So when I refer to the kids, I love to refer to them as "awesome kids." Who wouldn't want the label of awesome? I'm pretty sure we can let that "label" stick for a while.

The Power of Intention

As you can see, what we truly did by shedding our labels was to set strong intentions. Neither Michael nor I wanted to live in a paradigm of "I'm sick" any longer. Because we have free will, we had both strongly decided this. When you decide something strongly in this way, there is no stopping the manifestation. The key is being truly and fully aligned with the choice. If there is one little smidgen of doubt, a question, or a feeling of being "not worthy" of healing, then more work needs to be done to be fully aligned with your intention. Most times, when we don't accomplish our goal it is because of these other thoughts and distractions. That is when we really need to get down and dirty and figure out where this self-sabotage is coming from.

One thing I have noticed very strongly in the autism community is a huge power to manifest. Two years ago, a new biomedical protocol came out for treating parasites. Many families jumped on board head first doing this protocol. They have reported many "recoveries" from this.

This pattern sounded awfully familiar to me as I've been around the autism block for over 10 years now. In my healing practice, nearly every mother asked me to check whether this protocol was right for their child.

One day, I felt a very strong presence, that of Archangel Raphael coming through to explain this to me. Archangel Raphael is known as the "healing angel" and can be called upon for advice about healing the physical body. Here is his message:

Tami, this protocol has nothing to do with the actual substance being ingested. It has to do with the power of intention, the manifestation, the prayers that are strongly amplifying the healing energy in these families. It should be no surprise as we look back at the history of the autism community. Many children recovered just from simple dietary changes. A huge momentum built in the community after that first mother spread the world so boldly to her friends. People believed, they hoped, they dreamed that their child could heal too. And they did, many of them. Then other treatments came through like TD-DMPS, MB12-injections and so on. Each method brought recoveries and then a huge surge of momentum from the community. People believed. When they believed, they created.

Yet, what if someone gave the treatment and didn't believe, maybe they had fear or worry about its safety? Then no healing was done, and in some cases harm. What if the child didn't want to heal? Then the treatment didn't work because the child, even though a minor in age, still has free will choice and it is fully his choice whether to heal or not.

Just as there are thousands of mothers manifesting healing in their child, this can be done just as powerfully by the one mother all by herself. It's because she really isn't alone. If it is in the highest good for all involved and the child has decided he wants to fully heal, that momentum along with her guides, angels and her divine power can create healing as all is aligned in that direction. In her divine power she can call on the power of Jesus, thousands of angels or light beings to assist in this manifestation of healing. If it is to be, then it will be!

Another point is that to heal, one does not need any physical substance. The body and everything is energy so all healing can be done with energy as well. The miracles you hear about are usually these random healings that doctors cannot explain. That is energy based. This is not to discount the energetic hits one may receive with an idea for a supplement or treatment. This is usually given at a stage of development in the belief system of the parent. The parent believes that healing comes through doing or giving something, so the inspiration is delivered through that method. But truly one doesn't need any of that. The frequency of healing can be matched and delivered, and healing happens.

My point is that you don't need to spend thousands of dollars on treatments, leaving scars on your bank account and scars in your marriage if you understand this concept. Examine why you feel your child is not perfect. Isn't he already perfect? In the physical journey, the experience is perfect for all that we need to learn and realize in our lives. It is all perfect in every sense. Join me in discovering the perfection of your journey and all the gifts that it brings for the deepest love for all of you. Ask me to bring you gifts to your awareness so you can examine your beliefs and how they may have held you back in truly seeing the perfection in it all.

When I read Archangel Raphael's words, it rang so true as to what I have seen about the "treatment of the year" with autism. When the positive momentum fades out, so does the number of recoveries reported. I am not one that is crazy about the word recovery because I don't believe any of our kids are not perfect already. The lack of communication is perfection for some children. It is who they want to be, and where they are happy. It is our own beliefs and notions that cause us to look at them as damaged. They are not damaged, they are not victims. If we see them in this way, then they will also view themselves in that light. Hence, self-injurious behavior can come as a result of feeling less than or damaged. Your viewpoint, your words, and your thoughts can have a powerful impact on how your child sees themselves.

On the outside, it may look like a child is deeply suffering. That may be the case, but it isn't always so. It is more of a mirror reflection of what we feel on the inside. If you feel sorry or bad for a child and see them as suffering and it affects you, look deep into your own life and discover if in fact it is YOU that is suffering instead. Again, these children are in our lives to teach us and help us too. Much of that is seeing the truth of our own patterns. mantra says, "As I heal, others heal." As you wʊ⸴ your stuff, it frees up the space for your child to make choices about their healing.

I'm reminded of the work of Masaru Emoto, a researcher from Japan who recently passed away. He was able to take photographs of ice crystals from all kinds of water. In his pictures he is able to show the difference in the structure of water that has been prayed upon versus one that is exposed to hateful words. The difference is profound! I encourage you to read his book, *The Hidden Messages in Water*, and look up various You Tube videos on the topic. It will help you understand the power that your words, thoughts, and intentions hold.

Dr. Emoto's work will verify in a physical way how our intentions are manifested. He shows it through the element of water. If you understand the importance of water in our body, then you will see how the shift and change of our words, thoughts and intentions can then have a physical impact on the body.

Another point about our intentions is that sometimes our programmed beliefs chime in and sabotage our efforts. We say things on the inside like...

- It's impossible
- There is no way
- It's so hard
- We never catch a break

These beliefs LIMIT the ability to manifest. There is no good way to say it other than to say that one must shut these beliefs down. There are energy healing techniques to do that. One is called "Core Beliefs" in which I learned from Joy Gardner, the author of *Vibrational Healing through the Chakras*. This session is very powerful, and if you go on her website, you find a certified vibrational healer to work with you on this. www.highvibrations.net.

When we shed these old beliefs, something amazing happens. We open up to the ancient belief that "ANYTHING IS POSSIBLE." We will talk more about this later. When you start to play devil's advocate as to why something won't work, remember my words. Anything is possible and anything can happen!

Reversing What Isn't Working

It may seem so simple, even flippant at times, but if something isn't working for you, then reverse it! Let's say your child always wants to play on the iPad. If you take it away, they tantrum. You question if they are addicted to it. Although you know the EMF's are bad, it keeps your child calm. Each time your child tantrums for the iPad you give in and give it to them. Does the tantrumming stop? Yes, but temporarily, as you have set up a pattern of tantrum equals iPad. So this little dance you are both doing isn't really working out well (depending on who you ask). One solution would be to reverse it. Anytime you want to change a set in pattern, you have to throw something different into the energy pattern to break it up. You

need to do something differently from what you did before that contributed to the pattern. In this case, you cannot give the iPad. See what happens. I don't know the outcome here, but I do know that you would have shifted that pattern in some way.

Here's another example. My son loves to get food from Chipotle and take it to school. I'm ok with the food at Chipotle and his body handles it well. Yet, he got locked into a pattern of having to have Chipotle every time. What if I wanted to go to Veggie Grill instead? Nope...we had to go to Chipotle. Because I saw this as a growing pattern that quite honestly was annoying the hell out of me, I choose to reverse it. I periodically will change it up and say...nope we are going to Veggie Grill today. He hems and haws for a while and then accepts and we are all good. He says I try to stir the pot sometimes and yes, he is certainly right. That is because I don't want him to get so locked in the pattern that he can't see out.

Write down some of the negative patterns that go on in your home. What can you do to reverse them or throw some new energy into the pattern to change it up? Just work on one pattern at a time. You wouldn't want to change things too quickly as it could really cause some disruption in the home. Go slow and easy, doing one at a time. It may even take weeks to resolve one pattern, but be sure to be consistent with it. If you find another pattern forming that is negative, then you would want to adjust and change that up as well. So be flexible in your approach. Also be intuitive with your approach because some patterns that are annoying to us are important to our children. They may be receiving a benefit they need such as comfort, nurturing, safety and love. So if you feel this negative pattern also has positive benefits then look deep inside yourself to determine if it is in the highest good for all for it to change. It may be perfect as is.

What lesson am I supposed to learn here?

I have found a very effective technique for staying balanced even when seemingly hard or crappy things are happening. I ask myself, "What lesson am I supposed to learn here?"   It helps me to shift out of the victim mode and right into the learning and empowerment mode. It seems so simple, yet when we are stuck in our mind thoughts we tend to shut down our ability to see the lesson.

When my brother died, we were very much stuck in the why zone. Why would he kill himself? Why was he depressed? We had so many questions and so few answers. We spent so much effort trying to piece it all together so we could understand. Yet later, much later, it is clearer. You see, my brother was bullied in school, not every day, but just enough to make his life miserable. He usually had just a few close friends he could trust and stuck close to them. But does one truly know the damage that bullying can do? For my brother, I believe it was just one of those things that chips away at your confidence, little by little until you question your self-worth. Then you may settle for situations that may not be the best for you because you feel you don't deserve any better. You may trick yourself into believing you are happy but you are really living in a fantasyland you created by making choices from a disempowered place.

To bring him to the brink of suicide was not an overnight task. Years of these patterns, hidden away, masked with a bravely stubborn demeanor, is what fooled himself and his family into believing it didn't exist. Then the day came when he was rejected so publicly that the shame could no longer be hidden. That was the tipping point and no turning back for him. Could we see it in the moment? Absolutely not. But when?

It wouldn't be until years later. For me, it came nearly 25 years after his death when I was able to communicate with him in Spirit. He shared how he couldn't do the work he could in his body. He can make more of a difference from his spiritual form. He explained how he has planted certain ideas in my family, as flower seeds, to eventually blossom and bloom. They did when my parents founded the SACK Foundation which stands for Simple Acts of Care and Kindness. Their primary project is to educate 4th graders about bullying, so they can understand the bully and help those that seem to attract bullying. They have touched the lives of thousands of children over the years. Would that have happened without my brother and his story? I can say with certainty, no. When you think about it, this is huge!

But it took me awhile to get what we were supposed to learn here. Now that I understand how every experience we have is a lesson, I can utilize that much more quickly in the day to day. One thing I now understand is that NOTHING IS A MISTAKE. The concept of mistake is also an illusion. Something may not turn out as we had hoped, but it is not a mistake, it is a lesson. Some lessons come easier than others.

Certainly many in the autism community have learned some lessons the hard way. Many mothers have shared with me that at the moment the pediatrician was to give their child vaccines, their intuition shouted at them, "STOP!" But their mind came in and said "You're not a doctor, be quiet, this is best." And they let it happen. These moms tell me that they knew, but they didn't feel empowered enough to speak up and stop it. The lesson is to always honor your intuition. That is the lesson that likes to show up many times until we fully start living that concept. I still get that lesson from time to time.

Isn't it interesting how that parallels my brother's story? It's close to the same thing…the person not feeling empowered enough to demand something different for their life. Then tragedy strikes.

Another thing I have observed is how many doctors have children diagnosed with autism. What is the lesson there? How many beliefs have they needed to shed in order to help their child? (Probably half of what they learned in medical school.)

Some of us have gotten really good at spotting the lessons for others. We see our friends eating junk food, getting cancer and just know that there are lessons they aren't seeing. We can do as my brother does and plant seeds, but we can't make them understand the lesson. We can honor their journey even if it feels like they are moving stubbornly slow. We must honor their process of discovery and allow them to experience their lessons at their pace. It's not our journey to live, it's theirs.

I bring this up because it is very difficult for many in the autism community to live out in the real world (outside of autism). It's because we see the destruction, the chemicals, the unmindful behavior towards the environment and others. But it's not our job to change them, it's their job to change themselves. Remember to neutralize yourself and allow them to experience the lessons...and plant a few seeds of information along the way. Know that it is up to them to grow and nurture those seeds or mow over them.

What lessons have you learned from your experience with autism? How have you changed because of these lessons? I ask you to do this exercise so you can see things in a different way. Often times we shift into the thoughts of what is bad or hard and have a hard time seeing the blessings.

"The most amazing journey on earth is the journey of oneself."

-Lailah Gifty Akita

Chapter 12:
High Vibrational Healing

I hope that if you've read this far into the book, you have realized that not everything that looks dysfunctional on the outside really is. Some things are part of our path, our lessons and our purpose. Yet, what our body, mind and spirit is always looking for is balance. I look at balance in a very unique way. Balance to me is neutral. Balance is the zero point. Balance is aligned. Balance is at one. Vibrational healing strives to do just that, bring one into balance. We cannot begin to assume that we are smarter than the divine essence, so using an intuitive approach to bringing tools in to help shift one into balance is really the only acceptable method.

Everything in this world, our thoughts, our emotions and anything we can even imagine IS energy. With the power of intention, one can send vibrational frequencies to themselves or another with just an intent. No need to purchase items. Usually only very advanced healers claim to do this, yet that thinking only brings up a belief of "I'm not good enough" to many people which is harmful to perpetuate. All beings have this capability. The challenge is remembering that you are awesomely capable of doing this. Until you remember this, you can use the actual substance, as intuitively guided, to bring about balance to yourself and your family.

One thing I am very excited about is called Innerwise©. Dr. Uwe Albrecht, a pioneer in energy medicine from Germany has developed a simple, at-home method in which one can diagnose energetic imbalances through the "arm length test" and then intuitively select the frequencies to balance the issue. I was spiritually guided to this method and will be teaching the Innerwise healing method in the United States to parents who would like to learn and use this in their home. I will also be teaching practitioners how to use the more advanced techniques in their practice and receive life changing results in their clients. As in all successful energy healing approaches, one must:

1. Uncover the hidden cause.

2. Discover why the issue is there.

3. Learn what is needed to balance the issue.

An intuitive may just "receive" the answers and be able to move forward from there. Whereas most people need methods in order to uncover the answer until they are more able to receive clear guidance. The Innerwise arm length test is another form of muscle testing that can help one find the answers.

Muscle Testing

I have taught muscle testing successfully for years and hundreds have been able to learn the basic techniques. The idea is that by using certain movements in the body one can detect a stress response or a balance response.

The question can also be asked in a yes or no question. With muscle testing, the body will let you know how it feels about a certain substance or idea by responding. Muscle testing skips over the logical mind, beliefs and opinions when done appropriately. The answers are received from the subconscious or unconscious mind which is connected to Spirit where all answers are known. The body's response is your answer.

Pretty much anything can be asked via muscle testing. One can test foods, supplements, medications, ideas, colors, what to wear, allergies, etc. It is not recommended to ask questions of the future because the future is fluid and decisions we make today can change the future outcome. You would only be seeing the future by the perspective of today's reality.

To learn muscle testing, you can take my online course. This teaches the basics for the at-home healer and is not a professional course. This can be found online at: www.EpiphanyHealingArts.com/muscle_testing_made_easy.html.

For practitioners, I would recommend learning Autonomic Response Testing (ART) from Dietrich Klinghardt, MD. You can find more information at:
www.KlinghardtAcademy.com

The most important thing to remember with muscle testing is that you must practice. The more you practice, the more your confidence builds, and you will see how this can be the most valuable skill you could ever learn for your family.

Meditation

Meditation can bring about the next level, the level after muscle testing. This is how we receive spiritual guidance. As we quiet our mind and breathe deeply, we can allow our crown chakra to open and receive messages from our spirit guides and helpers. I don't believe in any one type of meditation. As you can probably tell, I don't like locking myself in a box of it having to be this way or that. But for my own personal practice, it looks very much like me relaxing, laying down and breathing slowly and peacefully. I may set an intention of something to work on, but ultimately I am just open to receiving whatever is supposed to be given to me.

As you slowly breathe, your thoughts can drift by you and release into the Universe. You can feel your vibration raising higher and higher. Your body may even begin to tingle, your hands becoming tingly and warm. This means you are right there in the place to receive. You may receive visions or insights, hear sounds, smell flowers or just feel an open-hearted, loving peace emanate through you.

I prefer to lie down, but however you are the most comfortable is the way you should do it. My recommendation is to carve out at least 30 minutes per day of non-negotiable time, just for you, to do this. Don't worry if you fall asleep. If you do, then I guess you needed a nap and all is good.

This is your time. There is no need to be the martyr and sacrifice your own peace in the name of fixing autism. I speak to your heart when I say that this will not serve either of you well at all. In fact, it's only when we can shift our own energy to a higher vibration that our awesome ones allow themselves to heal.

If you would like to experience some guided meditations with the focus on connecting with the awesome kids then I would recommend the World Autism Meditation recordings that can be found on my website. You will see that they are both for the children and for the adults and may be just what's needed to help you get in that peaceful state that we all crave so much.

Healing Tools

Now that you have some tools that will help you discover what the issue is and why it is there, what can you do to balance it? I've actually scattered a few methods throughout the book already, but I wanted you to know of some other great tools that can be used alone or in combination with each other.

Essential Oils

Ok, so I'm totally NOT going to get into a discussion about brand preference, multi-level marketing or anything like that. I am going to list some that I personally have been successful with and enjoy using in my home for my family and for my clients. I tend to use essential oils more for the vibrational properties than the physical properties. If you want to read which one kills bacteria, this is not the book. This is about what oil brings the healing vibration and how it can be used. When the appropriate healing vibration is entered into the energy field, the body can shift into a harmonic healing state. That is what we want.

Orange Essential Oil – This is a beautiful oil for bringing sunshine into your life. It can be used on the solar plexus topically or diffused/inhaled. This is particularly effective for those that are a little depressed, sluggish and need that extra oomph of energy. When you inhale orange it can give you sense of "All is right with the world." This is my happy oil. Diffuse orange oil and play "Happy" by Pharrell Williams and you can be on top of the world!

Patchouli Essential Oil – This has a very earthy fragrance. You may not like this scent, but it is because some people have a difficult time grounding. This is a grounding essence that helps balance the Root/Base Chakra. It is for people that have their head in the clouds so to speak and need to be brought back to Earth. This can be diluted in a carrier oil and rubbed on the bottoms of the feet or the tailbone area. It helps bring one back into their body in a gentle way.

Lavender Essential Oil – Vibrationally, it has many uses. I use lavender to bring calmness and serenity into the field. If one is jittery or highly emotional, this may be the vibration needed to relax the sensory overload that many experience. Even just a drop on a cotton ball, smelling it for a moment, can make a big difference. Lavender can also be rubbed on the base of the skull as a way to "loosen stuck thinking." I know a few men that could use that one!

Chamomile – I'm being guided to talk with you about chamomile, not necessarily in the essential oil form, but the herbal form. The vibration of chamomile is very beautiful. It seems to bring beautiful relaxation and a softening of the nerves. I have seen it bring relief to children with seizures whose brain seems to misfire often. This seems to calm the nervous system and is good for kids that are on "high alert."

Rose Water – Again, not sure why my guides are getting me off the track of the essential oil focus, but they are. Anyways, rose water, simple rose water that you can get in the cosmetics section of the Whole Foods Market will suffice. The scent of roses opens the heart chakra in a beautiful way. It helps to balance the giving and receiving of love and puts an energy in that raises that heart frequency in a beautiful way. For very stressful types of kids, this works like magic. For those that feel a bit depressed or negative, this can boost their energy. Think about how just smelling a rose in nature can make you feel. Spray that smell into the aura and you can really infuse that feeling into your energetic field, feeling that love all day long.

Healing Waters – Since I'm already off track of the essential oils, I might as well continue. Water can be infused with love, peace and joy with your beautiful intention

and become an amazing vibrational healing tool. A wonderful man named Robbie who I met at Angel Valley in
Sedona has developed an amazing water device for infusing vibration into the water. We have to stay tuned on
this one. Once it is available to the masses I will post it on
my website. The water he creates has the vibration of
Christ Consciousness and I would love to see it accessible
to everyone. But in the meantime, feel free to pray over
the water, bring in the light and infuse it with loving energy. The water may even change its taste and feel like
you are sipping an iceberg and be tingling to the tongue.
That is those high vibes! You can also spray the water into
the aura for a quick energy cleansing.

On the same theme as healing waters, sulphur springs, as
indicated, can also be very healing and a wonderful vibration, helpful in melting toxic emotions and physically aid-
ing the body in detox. Not all can tolerate the sulphur so
be sure to test it first.

There are hundreds of essential oils, and the blends that
can be created are numerous. To stay true to my process, I
only listed the ones in which the vibrational healing is
important for you to know about. If you decide upon a
brand of oils you like, then get their master list and learn
about their properties. Then when you are muscle testing
or using your intuition, it is likely that one of those will
pop up as just the exact frequency needed to balance that
issue. Understand that it seems odd that I didn't talk
about frankincense, my favorite oil. This is because it
tends to bring you out of your body and is excellent for
meditation. Yet, most awesome kids are already out of

their bodies much of the time, so frankincense n always be the best choice for some. But test it and s

If you don't have the oil, I want you to imagine you do have it in your hand. See yourself using that oil and infusing the frequency of that oil in the energetic field of your child. Test….did he receive it? You'll get a yes, and know that you can do this with anything and see the shift right in front of your eyes.

Flower Essences

Flower essences can be very powerful for emotional and mental issues. There are so many brands and many are very affective. Originally it started with Edward Bach creating the Bach Flower Essences, which are the most readily available flower essences. Flower essences are not made of actual flowers. They are the energy of the particular flower that is used to shift emotional issues. It is vibrational healing at its finest. The most well-known is called Rescue Remedy, which is used in times of trauma and grief very effectively. Flower essences can be used for children, adults and even our pets. You may use the Bach line successfully or feel drawn to Alaskan Essences, Bush Flower Essences, FlorAlchemy, or others.

One day, Michael came downstairs and told me of a dream he had. He said that the doorbell rang and there was an angel. The angel was surrounded in cherry blossoms. Then he woke up. He told me he felt the cherry blossoms were a message for him. As I connected with this issue it came to me to google cherry blossom flower essence. I found a company called One Willow Apothecary. When I read the description of the purpose for cherry blossom flower essence it matched perfectly for what he was experiencing emotionally. I ordered it and continue to order it as he uses it regularly. He said that anytime he feels a little "off" or not right about something, he puts a few drops in his water and feels 100% better.

Flower essences can have an instant healing effect. What is really beautiful is that you just can't mess these up. If you "misheard" guidance or were off in your muscle testing and gave your child the wrong one, nothing happens. The energy of the flower essence goes to those who need it, and not to those who don't. You can even have your child select the essences he wants to use. This is probably the most effective way because then they are aligned with the treatment and already accepting the vibration.

Homeopathy

This is a method of healing that one should consider if you are not seeing results with herbs, supplements or medications. Even better, find someone who practices *Intuitive Homeopathy* and they will have a more spiritually guided approach to healing. Become familiar with some of the basic remedies for homeopathy and you will be guided if needed to use these with your awesome kid. Homeopathy is natural, works with the energy of the body and can resolve imbalances at every level. Often times it goes to the root cause without the knowledge of what that cause is. There is value in the many forms of homeopathy. Classical, CEASE, sequential, homotoxicology and others have each proven to be highly effective. You can choose the best for your child by testing or allowing your intuition to guide you to a practitioner or method.

Reiki and Channeled Energy

In your search for the vibration that balances the issue, you may feel guided to explore Reiki or other energy healing techniques. Reiki is a channeled energy, guided by spirit. It means spiritually guided life force energy. A Reiki practitioner or Reiki Master may channel this energy to balance the chakras and heal imbalances in the body. It is very important that this person be "clean." If you begin to work with someone and they seem to speak in fear-based language, then I would run the other way. Anyone you work with should shine pure light from their being. You can pick it up by your first impression of that person. Since we are all human, we all can pick up on negativity at times and we all do. But if an energy healer isn't clearing and working on themselves, it can be counterproductive to the session. An energy healer should always vibrate unconditional love. If you feel you are being judged by him/her, then walk away.

That being said, energy healing can be off the hook amazing when it's the right fit. So test the practitioner you have in mind and see if you are aligned with that person. If so, then it's a beautiful match that is sure to bring beautiful healing for your family.

Nature Energy

Sometimes, just some time in nature is all it takes. When we connect with nature we are in tune with our true being. Imbalance no longer can be part of us when we are in full alignment. I would love to get into the spiritual beings in nature and how they help us on our path, but I want you to understand this simply.

The plants, animals, soil, sand, rocks, trees, water, oxygen, and carbon dioxide all make up nature. All of the elements make up nature: water, wind, Earth and fire. Nature can be mimicked in our bodies. Inflammation feels like fire. Scatterbrained thoughts feel like the wind, and so on. The energy of trees with their ancient roots can help us to bring our energy more into our bodies, connecting to the Earth. When we join in nature we agree to balance our own elements. As we spend time in nature, we connect with ourselves and that which is greater than just us.

One of my favorite places is the beach. I share this love with the majority of awesome kids. We are drawn to the beach because of the grounding energy of the sand, the cleansing breath of the wind and the joyful mystery of the whales and dolphins. At the beach we connect with our most primal and our most spiritual self. We feel free and connected. It is no wonder that children beg for time at the beach and many mothers report seeing a whole different child when they are in this environment.

The beach is so healing that even as the thought enters in my mind to go, I feel my entire body vibrate with the knowing that I'm going home. The body feels alive and in complete balance with just a few minutes near the energy of the beach.

This can be simulated in some way by being sure that your child knows how to swim. Children are drawn to the vibration of water and unfortunately many children have transitioned due to wandering near ponds and lakes without the skills to swim safely. Knowing why they want to be near the water is half the battle and ensuring he has adequate water time to help him come to balance will lessen his urge to explore on his own.

Sound Healing

There are many ways of creating a vibration through sound. Crystal bowls, Tibetan singing bowls, tuning forks, vocal toning, drumming, didgeridoo, the gong and others can be used to bring in a specific vibration. It does need to be specific though, as I myself have gone wacky when vibrations that were not appropriate for me to have been entered into my energy field. Some believe that sound frequency is the most innate method of communication in the spiritual realms. I have seen some truth in this as well. I recommend using sound healing for the lower chakras of the body as the vibration can sometimes be too intense around the head, causing a jitteriness or anxiousness in the nervous system.

Color

It is well known that color can affect our moods. We discussed color earlier, but I want to add on to that information. It is because it also holds a vibration. You would want to determine if a color would make your kid hyper wouldn't you? If you are mindful about the color selections then it can save you some sanity in the long run.

Red/Orange	passion, bringing in energy, excitement, loud, inflammation
Yellow	happy, sunshine, boost of energy, power, God-self
Green	healing, comfort, nature
Pink	sweet, soft, loving, gentle
Blue	relaxing, ocean, expressive, open, understanding
Violet	intuitive, knowing, protected
White	all colors, all properties, alive, divine light, effervescent, soothing
Black	open

There are also color antidotes that can be used. So if your child is acting super RED and it's too much, another color can be brought in to antidote the red.

Antidotes:
Red – Blue
Orange – Indigo
Yellow – Violet

The antidotes can be used to balance if there is an excessive color imbalance. Consider this when choosing the clothes, sheets, blankets and colors in the room. Each color should be mindfully considered for the individual awesome kid.

Crystals

Rocks, stones and crystals are absolutely amazing for vibrational healing. The energy can be felt by many just by holding a crystal in their hand. These are considered "sentient beings" where they are alive and able to emit a vibration for specific purposes. Crystals each have a purpose for being in this world and that can be used, with permission, for amazing healing. I recommend taking your child to a crystal shop and letting him choose his favorites. He will likely be drawn to them. He may want to hold them and even put them up to his face or head. He is reading and communicating with the crystal and determining if he is the one to work with this crystal. It is in his knowing that he remembers how to do this. Know that it doesn't matter the beauty of the crystal. So don't choose them based on their looks, only on their "feel."

One of my most powerful crystals I got for free from a tub of tumbled stones at the crystal shop. It was a blue sodalite. One day I woke up with a sore throat and was trying to figure out what to do. I was guided to put that little rock on my throat and then drive to work. In 15 minutes my sore throat was gone. Here are some of my favorite crystals for awesome kids...

Amethyst – use to connect with your intuition

Clear Quartz – very powerful when charged with good intention.

Smoky Quartz – used for clearing negative energy

Sugilite – my favorite for parents to use to open third eye chakra for clearer spiritual vison.

Black Obsidian – grounding stone

Black Tourmaline – grounding and clearing negative energy

Azurite – for opening up channels of verbal communication

Rose Quartz – use to bring love to a situation or to an area of the body.

Just like all of our other tools, there are many more to choose from. If your child chooses something not on this list, honor their choice. If you decide you like crystals then you may want to study them in more detail and learn different techniques on how to use them in your home, cleanse them and charge them.

Our Animals as Healing Friends

Oh yay, it's my favorite topic! I don't even know where to start. You wouldn't necessarily use your pet at a vibrational tool, although they can do this naturally, but I must mention to you the healing capabilities of our pets. Although I love cats, I am more of a dog person, so I am going to approach this subject that way.

When one becomes more aware of their spiritual gifts, you may notice something. Your dog is communicating with you too! He is doing it in the same way that a pre-verbal awesome kid does. There is a soul there and they have a soul purpose as well. Many animals come into our lives to help us. Start to notice the relationship your child has with your animals. Do they ignore each other? Do they have an unbreakable bond? I have seen animals rise up to be healers right in their own home. They bring their own set of experiences and lessons to us, just like our kids do.

When Mr. Pepper was going blind, he kept peeing in the upstairs hallway. He seemed to do it right in front of my husband. One day, I asked why he was doing that. He said, "I am showing Troy that he needs to be more mindful of me and the fact I can't see. He rushes around me and bumps into me. It's hard for me to know where I'm going when he does that." When I gave the message to my husband, he understood and became more mindful of his movements when around Pepper. The peeing stopped.

My dog Mac has started to poke me with his nose during client sessions. He's poking me and trying to flip my hand up so I'll pet him. One day I asked him, "Do you have a message for me?" He replied, "Yes...the boy you are working on is very sad." I said "Thank you" and Mac walked away to lie down. He was not only in tune with me, but the boy's energy as well.

Are our dogs and cats home healers too? Mac came to us as a service dog flunkee. He enjoyed chasing birds too much on his walks to do his service dog training effectively. I found it a bit funny that he is also sensitive to grains and needs a gluten-free diet. I wonder if he is an awesome kid in a dog's body. Anyways, one thing I wanted them to train Mac to do was to lay on Michael when he got agitated. Even with all the training in the world, Mac wouldn't do it. They marked the price of Mac down to 50% off and he came home with us. The first time Michael got agitated, Mac walked right over and laid his head on Michael's lap. Michael giggled and forgot all about why he was upset. Mac naturally and intuitively knew what to do. He didn't need training to teach him to be kind and loving to his boy, it's who he is. That is healing in my book!

We can't forget about the beautiful connections and stories told about horses and awesome kids. The deep awareness and in the moment presence they bring to each other is definitely divinely inspired as noted in the book The *Horse Boy*.

I believe even our pets are with us for a reason. What's the lesson here? Time to connect with them and find out.

Chapter 13:
Awakening to Your Gifts

When we bring these concepts, energies, and vibrations into our home and into daily practice, big shifts can happen. There seems to be more peace and understanding in the home. Compassion for each other flows freely. It is something we need to keep up with, as we are being pruned and taught new lessons that we must adjust to. There is one thing I know for sure, bringing the light into your home will cause shifts and overall have a positive impact. This journey is not without its struggles though. Isn't that what life is all about? We didn't come here to relax and lounge around (although that sounds awfully nice). We came here to learn and evolve. As you awaken to your soul purpose and spiritual gifts, those around you must shift in some way. Because we are all intertwined and connected, when one shifts, the other does too.

In my home this was pretty obvious in some ways, and then very minute in other ways. I'm don't mean to pick on my husband, but he is a slower mover than the rest of us when it comes to personal growth. That's ok with me. Thankfully, our awesome kid friend James helped me understand his role as divine as well, even if it looks more grounded and less spiritually guided. We all hold these roles for each other, and how they can benefit us gets revealed bit by bit over time. It is tempting to want to know it all now. What is going to happen? Will my child speak? Will he recover? Yet our journey needs to be followed in its divine timing so that the lessons can be revealed and learned along the way. It's not about the destination, it's all about the journey.

As you travel down this road of learning and opening more to your soul purpose you may find some interesting experiences happening. For me, when I took that first Reiki class, I had my first clairvoyant and clairaudient experience. I want to talk about these spiritual senses so you will understand what can happen.

Clairaudience: This is when you "hear" information from Spirit. This can be in the form of your spirit guides, angels, or any energetic being bringing you a message. It could sound like an exterior voice, as if you are talking on the phone, or it may sound like your own thoughts. Yet, the difference is that the words are not originating from you. So the words seem to "pop in" or come out of nowhere. This is the same sense used in the conversational type of telepathy. It's like a conversation is going on in your head. You may question and think you are crazy and making it up. But if you aren't creating it and it truly is popping in to your awareness, then it is true.

Clairvoyance: This is when you "see" information from Spirit. This is channeled through your third-eye chakra which is the area for inner vision. You may get a flash of a picture in your mind. You may have a lucid dream in which everything is very clear. This may seem like a daydream, but if there are relevant messages, then it is not from your imagination. Some see energy with their bare eyes. They see sparkles in the sky or the aura of people and animals. This is clairvoyance, and the information can be very useful.

Claircognizance: This is also known as "clear-knowing." This is the primary sense used in our intuition. It's that "gut feeling" for some or when you just "know" stuff. The truth is that the information we receive here may have also come via our other senses and delivered to you in a package of just knowing.

Clairsentience: This is a sense very known to empaths. This is when we feel the message. We may feel a sensation in our body which brings us the message. I used to feel the physical symptoms in my clients as a roadmap to provide me with the information needed to help them. Many awesome kids like to send messages via this pathway as do animals. The important thing here is to ask, "Is this MY symptom or someone else's?" Another interesting thing here is that you can train yourself to muscle test using this sense. Without moving a muscle you can notice your body response when in stress or when in balance. For example, when I am in stress I feel butterflies in my stomach. When I feel balance, I feel love flow from my heart. You might test this out with a few things and see what your signals are in your body.

One can also receive messages through scents that appear out of nowhere. Just the other day, Michael and I were in the car and we both smelled the strong scent of cough drops. We rolled down the windows to see if it was coming from outside, and it wasn't. I heard in my mind (clairaudience), it's Grandma Dee Dee. I then asked if she had a message for me and she did. So, two senses were used during that episode.

Another way we can receive messages is through songs. Have you ever had a song stuck in your head that came in out of nowhere? This is a daily occurrence for me. Next time, look at the lyrics and see if there is something you need to learn from the lyrics. Sometimes our relatives who have passed send us songs just to say hi to us from the spirit world.

We can also receive messages through nature. The Shamans believe that when animals come into our awareness they bring messages and guidance to us. I have seen this to be true. If you want to learn more about this, I recommend the book, *Animal Spirit Guides*, by Stephen Farmer. I have received messages from all kinds of animals. The key is to be open to receive those messages.

Humans can also be powerful messengers of guidance. I see this all the time. We don't even know it when we are the messenger. What happens is that we say or type the words that are just the thing the receiver needs to know at the time. This could be anything from a specific treatment idea or words of encouragement. We play this role as messenger and receiver all the time. If you find that you are aware that you are the messenger, be sure not to become attached to any outcome. People can take it or leave it. Your job is to deliver. Their openness to receive is their path, not yours.

Knowing how guidance can come to you is important. Don't worry about missing something. I've found that if the message is important, it may come to you many times so you "get it."

Letting Go

By now you may have realized that this autism journey is as much about you as it is your child. In order to raise your vibration to create this awakened home, we find ourselves being called to do some pretty deep inner-work. Inner-work is basically cleaning up the old stuff, taking care of your business to make room for new, more vibrant living.

Letting go of the past is an important part of this. We tend to hold on to our "story" and tell the same one over and over again. I talk to parents and they tell me all about the horrible symptoms their child has. When I probe though, many times those symptoms aren't even present any-more. The child is in a different state. Yet, the mom is still living in the injury of what happened, how terrible it was and how traumatic it was for everyone. This is when we must work to heal those old traumas. When we heal the old traumas we are creating space for a new reality. If we perpetuate the thoughts of trauma, victim, and disease then that is what we experience now.

Here's an exercise in letting go. You may want to memo-rize it ahead of time so you aren't distracted trying to read as you go. Or you can record this into your phone,

ly, taking a 1-2 minute pause between the activi-
ve yourself enough time and space to do this.

1. Get in a quiet space, close your eyes and take some nice deep breaths. (10 slow breaths please.)

2. Ask to be shown the areas in your body where you store grief.

3. Ask your guides to send light there and help you release the grief energy. Breathe.

4. Ask to be shown the areas in your body where you store anger.

5. Ask your guides to send light there and help you release the anger energy. Breathe.

6. Ask to be shown the areas in your body where you store resentment.

7. Ask your guides to send light there and help you release the resentment. Breathe.

8. Ask to be shown the areas in your body where you show fear.

9. Ask your guides to send light there and help your release the fear. Breathe.

10. Ask your guides to send light to soften any part of you showing resistance. Breathe.

11. Feel the light flowing through you. Enjoy the peace here for a while. When you are ready, come back into your body awareness and open your eyes.

12. Journal any experiences you had.

As we store anger and resentment, our body holds it in a form of cellular memory. When we come across a similar experience, we are then triggered back to a time when we felt that way too. In order to release at the cellular level, sometimes we need to do something physical to let it go. Here are some suggestions, and strangely enough, most involve the use of a pillow...

- Scream into a pillow.
- Sing in the shower.
- Cry while you are swimming in the pool.
- Cry in a pillow.
- Punch the pillow.
- Use the pillow to smack the crap out of the bed.
- Walk it off and imagine each footstep releasing the crud into the Earth.
- Punch a punching bag or heavy bag.
- Workout with the intention of releasing negative emotions as you sweat.

There are all kinds of things you can do. When I learned Vibrational Healing from Joy Gardner, we did emotional release work by using these flexible hard rubber tubes and smacking the crap out of a yoga mat. It was very effective. The key here is to allow the emotion to bubble up as if you are back in it, then as you move your body, the emotions are purged from the cells. As you cry, yell or scream it is released even more. If it is difficult to cry, then you are usually holding back and wanting to hold on to these emotions. If that were the case, look into why you would want to hold on to them. Is there some benefit for you? What could the benefit be of holding on to anger? It may be something that deeply needs to be looked at because if one is holding on to anger purposely, it may be that one is trying to punish another or oneself. If that's the case, then the relationship and karma there needs to be examined.

If you are ready to let go of something, I want you to go back to a time where you felt you or your child was victimized. How did you feel? Feel those emotions begin to bubble and now let's let it go. It served its purpose, and now it's time to move on. After any emotional release session, be sure to call in the light to infuse and balance you with healing vibrations, and you will be nurtured and supported right to the end.

Forgiveness

To forgive is not to forget. It is to release ourselves of the suffering we have implored upon ourselves as we hold on tightly to our position. Is our position being the victim? Forgiveness is not allowing the same thing to happen again. Forgiveness is the ultimate freeing force so we can be alive and in our power again.

We can use the practice of Ho'oponopono to help us to forgive. In this practice one is to take responsibility for our part in what we experience. As we view others as mean, damaged, or suffering, we are called to look at those aspects within our own self. I choose to see the spiritual brilliance in our awesome kids, and not see them as suffering or diseased.

Because I choose that, in my presence with them, they show me this part of them. If it's a mirror, then I am also seeing my own divine brilliance through them.

To me, the ultimate forgiveness is to notice this and shift it. It is with these simple words that true forgiveness of others and self can be realized through Ho'oponopono. Remember we talked about it before, here is the mantra:

I'm sorry
Please forgive me
I love you
Thank you

You can chant this mantra whenever you experience negativity that seems aimed towards you. To release it, you have to understand that what you are experiencing, you may also be putting out there to others. Imagine the person or entity (say the CDC or Monsanto) and chant this, send it to them. Do it over and over until you feel the shift. The shift happens in you and in them. In our inter-

energy we can grow together. This may seem so
nd even silly when you try it at first. As you con-
unue to do this, you will start to see the difference.

If you have been holding anger and resentment towards
someone and know that the time has come to forgive, I
have found a three-fold approach to be affective.

1. **Send forgiveness to the person, fully and completely.** (I forgive you for _____ fully and
   completely from all levels of my being.)

2. **Send forgiveness to yourself.** (I forgive myself for
   holding on to these emotions for so long and allowing this to impact my life and others.)

3. **Send forgiveness to others involved.** (I forgive
   anyone else for their part in this situation. I release
   any negative emotions and give unconditional forgiveness to the situation.)

Please understand that it doesn't matter whether someone receives your forgiveness or not, physically. Their
higher self and soul will receive it easily. If you put it out
there, they will get it and it is released from you. Remember, forgiveness isn't a free pass to cause harm to another
or yourself, it is simply a way to release you of the torture
of your own anger and resentment. It's an e-ticket to freedom!

Shedding Old Beliefs

I find our beliefs to be absolutely fascinating. Let's look at medical marijuana for example. For decades we have been taught that it is a dangerous drug, and that it is a gateway to more serious drug abuse like cocaine, etc. Many looked down upon those who used marijuana, labeling them "pot heads," etc. The belief system that marijuana is harmful is deeply embedded in American society.

Yet, someone found benefit in it for their physical body for glaucoma, cancer, seizures and other physical ailments by making it into an oil. Most still snubbed their nose at it, until those ailments showed up at their house. Then their belief system began to shift. Maybe they could give it a try. Then miracles happened. More and more people, little by little, began to shift out of the belief that it was bad. Now, new beliefs are forming that it is healing and therapeutic. A movement across the country to legalize medicinal marijuana is surging through the nation! The beliefs are shifting!

In the whole autism world there have been many societal beliefs that have shifted in this community. How about these...

- Doctor knows best.
- All children need to receive vaccines to be safe.
- Genetically modified food is safe.
- The government protects us from harmful chemicals.

I'm pretty sure that if you are reading this book, then you have shed the above beliefs. Yet, these beliefs are ingrained in much of our society. It took experiences in your life for you to shift these beliefs and create new ones.

What about the beliefs we have about ourselves. We carry these beliefs from childhood and they can become the mental tapes that run in the background of our mind, hindering us from growing and living our soul purpose. Here are some examples...

- I am worthless
- I am sick
- I am ugly
- I am no good
- I am mean
- I am high maintenance
- No one accepts me
- I can't manage money well
- I am broke
- I am a procrastinator
- I am dumb
- I am lazy
- (The list goes on and on.)

How did we get any of these beliefs? Did we create them ourselves? Oftentimes, they are created by someone we know. Usually, our family or people we have met in our lives have made comments to us about ourselves and implant these in our subconscious. If we were stronger in our power, then they would not hold. But as we experience trauma and hurt, we allow them in. The good news is that you can uncover these beliefs and change them! The most effective technique I know is through guided trance called Core Belief Work. The website lists practitioners who are specifically trained in this technique. www.highvibrations.net. Only use someone who has been certified to do this work. It is not for someone unqualified to do because we are reprogramming the subconscious beliefs, which is sensitive work.

The recognition that you still hold these beliefs is half the battle. You can make a conscious effort to shift them yourself. Try this:

1. Make your list of beliefs.

2. Where did they come from? Who and what experiences contributed to these beliefs?

3. Use the forgiveness technique from the previous section for each person and each belief.

4. Create new beliefs by reversing the old ones. (Even if you don't believe the new belief yet.)

5. Use the techniques we learned about in the affirmation section to infuse the new beliefs into your energy field.

You are fully supported

In times of struggle, it certainly may not feel like you have much support. But know that you are. We usually look for support from the outside, but know that we are supported in many unseen ways.

To give you an example, my Grandma Dee Dee gave Michael and me this visitation last week and delivered a message. Her message to me was to separate myself from an acquaintance of mine. She said that her energy was not positive for me to be around at this time, and I didn't need to spend so much effort balancing myself when around her. I should just let her go for a while. I felt very supported and almost like Grandma "had my back" when she gave me this message.

Then to make the point even further, last night I was given a dream. In the dream, I was in this long kayak out in the ocean with many people. As we were riding around, I saw a baby elephant swimming in the water. I screeched out with glee. After all, who would expect to see an elephant in the ocean? Then I saw a blackness right behind the elephant and soon realized it was a giant (at least 20 feet long) Great White shark approaching the elephant with its jaws wide open. We all screamed and I hid my face as I knew what was to happen. I screamed out in sheer horror and despair as to what was happening. As we floated in the bloody waters, they turned the kayak around to go back to shore. I was in the front of the kayak and was so unstable that as I tried to steady myself and not tip the boat, but I panicked even more and nearly tipped the boat. I tried to be stable but kept rocking it. Then this man behind me wrapped his arms around my core and said, "I've got you, let me steady you." For the rest of the ride, I was calm, stable, and we didn't tip over.

As I awoke, I still felt the grief for the elephant, even though my cognitive mind knows the circle of life and all of that. But what stood out to me was the message. Support can come in unexpected ways, from strangers, from friends, from family and even from our spiritual friends. Even when we see no support in site, it is still there, and there are those that are helping you keep steady and stay on course.

My dream is filled with metaphors. Was the shark autism? Was the baby elephant our kids in the way of harm? I don't know, I'm sure the answer is yes and no. It just reminds me how difficult as a parent it can be to stay calm and steady when you watch someone being attacked or if you are being attacked.

In 2014, a huge event hit the autism community. A whistleblower from the CDC came forward and gave information confirming what we already suspected, that the CDC had manipulated the results of vaccine studies to show no correlation to autism. To have someone directly involved tell the truth was absolutely huge. The community went wild getting this information out to the masses. It became what I call the Whistleblower Storm of 2014 because in retaliation came many attacks back at our community. This is a little article I wrote at that time that I want to share. It applies to any situation in our lives when we feel like we are falling out of balance and need to come back and steady ourselves.

How to Manage Our Emotions during a CDC Whistle-blower Storm
(Or any other big issue for that matter)

As many of us know someone or even gave birth to someone who was negatively affected by vaccines, the recent information being revealed about falsified studies released by the CDC has unleashed some major emotions in the autism community. These emotions are based on trauma or many traumas that we have experienced by watching physical, emotional, mental and spiritual pain in these children. Our intuition told us the truth many times over. But now we are on the verge of real scientific proof as Dr. Thompson's heart had softened and he claims he could no longer live with this information knowing they manipulated data on the 2004 MMR and autism study.

So our warrior spirits rise to fight. We want the information out there. We want people to listen. We want the CDC to admit what they did and how they could have prevented so much trauma in these children. But it falls on deaf ears. Once again, even with proof, the community is labeled (just as the children are labeled) and pushed aside as ranting, crazy mothers (and some fathers). Our emotions of feeling once again separate from the world, unheard, different, weird and feeling judged by the mainstream rise to the surface. Have you ever dreamed you were yelling at someone and they couldn't hear you? That's what it feels like now.

Zooming out to the big picture perspective we know many things. We know that we don't have to punish anyone as the Universe and Karma takes care of that. We know there are good people out there that want to speak up but are scared. And we know staying silent isn't the best way to go. But we also know that we run the risk of ostracizing the world if we come on too strong. Where is the balance?

The balance is in keeping ourselves neutral. We don't need to prove anything to anyone because we KNOW. We may feel like we want to save the other babies though. Let's look at it though....since this study in 2004 there have still been THOUSANDS of mothers screaming at the top of their lungs about this vaccine. And hundreds of thousands of mothers didn't listen. Many will say they intuitively felt something was off about giving the vaccines but didn't feel strong enough to say anything or refuse them. There is a lesson there. Many need to learn to trust their intuition, listen to that inner voice and be strong. It is not for us to teach them that lesson. Life will bring them the experience in some way or another if that is a life lesson they are here to learn. Many of us learned that one the hard way.

We can educate, be strong, listen to our intuition and be balanced, loving, compassionate, vibrant, sensitive, warrior mamas. If you feel like you have shifted out of that energy I just named, then here are a few tips...

1. Every morning, go outside barefoot and take 10 deep breaths. Breathe in the beauty of nature. Send your gratitude to your higher power. Feel your feet connecting to the Earth, grounding you, and feel the energy flow through your body with your crown of your head connecting to God.

2. Take some time in silence to balance your thoughts. Do this through meditation, prayer, soft music, or just lounging around. As your thoughts spin around recognize the thought. (Oh, I just thought about food) and so on. Breathe in and send the relaxing power of the breath through each cell in your body.

3. If you are sensitive to other energy, a worrier, or an empathetic person, then imagine you have a beautiful white light above your head and breathe the light into your body until it fills all your cells, all of your aura, all of your being. Imagine that light creating a protective shield around your entire aura. You can release things out, but no other energy can come in. It's your safe little cocoon. Feel it, imagine you can see it, and know that it is there.

4. At night as you take your shower, imagine rinsing all of the "yuck" emotions, thoughts, energy or whatever isn't serving you or supporting peace in your life. Imagine rinsing that down the drain. As you emerge from the shower you are clean, refreshed and at peace.

If you find yourself getting emotional often... repeat any or all of the above. And always remember to have compassion for all beings, even those that have done things we feel are wrong. We don't need to punish, as the Universe will always strive for balance in whatever way that comes. Sending love and light to all that read this.

When we make efforts to keep ourselves balanced we can be much more effective in getting people to listen and understand us. When we enter into the warrior phase too harshly, we come off as aggressive and full of rage. Even the most open minded person would not be receptive to that. My point is that in order to really feel and be supported, we need to be in an energetic state where we attract that support. Our receptivity is key here. In my dream, what would have happened if I refused the support of that man in the boat? We may have tipped over? I may have become more agitated. When support comes your way, it is the Universe bringing you balance, and receiving that support is a gift that we give to the giver. Just as when you give support to others, it brings balance to them and to you.

Let's look at it. Ask yourself these questions:

1. How are you at receiving compliments?
2. Do you prefer to do things your way?
3. Can you accept gifts from others graciously without feeling like you need to run out and get them a gift in response?
4. Do you always try to pay the dinner bill and not let others ever pay?

The Universe is always trying to balance. So if you are blocking yourself from accepting others help, then you're giving and receiving is out of balance and you will feel drained in your life. You will need to find ways of shifting it. The most important thing is your awareness on this and taking steps to either give more or receive more.

Some of this pattern comes to us through family patterns and other times it is an issue of trust. We feel like we can do it much better and don't trust anyone to help us. History may have proven you right but what also happens is we prevent ourselves and our children from new learning experiences where they can learn to adjust to a different way. Are we being inflexible, and then we see inflexibility in our children? If we were flexible and accepted support from others, would your child then be able to be more flexible as well?   Here we come back to the mirror pattern that is intertwined in much of our world. It's something to think about.

Uncovering Blocks

Some of us may feel blocked. It can be in many forms, but possibly a block to hearing your intuition or maybe even a block to deeply connecting to your child. You can uncover these blocks and learn to balance them. In the *Family Awakenings for Awesome Kids* home study course available on my website, we dig into this deeply with guided meditation and techniques to uncover those blocks. The truth is that you already know what they are and if you take the time to recognize them you can have a deeper understand of their source of creation.

Physical Blocks – This is anything in the physical body preventing you from connecting from your child. For this type of question, it would be rare to find a block originating in the physical field. Although fatigue could show up in this field, as well as another person who doesn't allow your help with the child and wants to do it all themselves. This block may show up in the fathers who feel impotent to help with the daily activities of the child.

Mental Blocks – This is your mental mindset, how you think about things. It is also your beliefs. Do you believe you can connect? Do you believe you are worthy of such a skill? Do you believe in yourself? Are religious beliefs or those of your family hindering your connection?

Emotional Blocks – This is where fear, anger, resentment, sadness, shame, trauma, and other emotions can show up and block you from achieving your goal/intention.

Spiritual Blocks – Ask the question: Is it in my highest good to connect in this way with my child? Is it my soul purpose? Is my soul aligned with this? Does something feel off but you can't pinpoint it? Is there a fear or emotion attached to a past life experience?

Other Patterns – Family patterns, DNA, miasms, ancestral, etc.

Once you uncover where these blocks exist, you can use muscle testing or vibrational healing to determine what you need in order to balance it. Any of the things we discussed such as homeopathy, flower essences, or energy work, can achieve balance and removal of these blocks. Ask the question...

What do I need to heal these blocks?

Allow the answer to be revealed to you. It will come to you in one way or another. Your job is to be receptive to the message arriving in whatever way it comes. It may be a quick pop of an idea, a dream, a Facebook post or some other way. Yes...even our spirit guides find ways to use social media to connect!

Energy Healing

Truly all that is vibrational healing is energy healing. One can utilize many techniques to bring healing vibrations into our energy field. Last year, though I was guided to create something, I had quite the waiting list for new clients and was feeling guilty about not being able to work with all that were seeking healing. In a beautiful meditation, the concept of Group Healing was given to me. All of the details and structure were given to me in just five minutes from my guides. It has truly been a blessing for many as it has brought peace and balance to many families.

Here is one mother's story about the healing she received that was part of our group healing program:

Mercury Poisoning and a Miracle Cure

When I came to the U.S., I was vaccinated with four different vaccines all together in the month of September, 1993. Three weeks later, everything began to go blurry. I could not see without my newly acquired glasses, and could not understand why my eyesight had suddenly deteriorated. Confusion reigned supreme. On coming out of my new apartment, I felt disoriented and could not remember which direction I needed to go to get to the laundry.

I could not remember anything. I had crying spells for no reason at all. Fast forward twenty-one years and a couple of months. I am into my eighth month of my homeopathic treatment and I begin to get pain in my heart. I had just joined Tami Duncan's healing group a scant few weeks ago. As if it were designed to, I thought to myself that there was no way I would ever have a psychic experience like a mom on Tami's Facebook group described. I could not even bring up the memory of being taught that.

I suddenly felt an intense pressure arising from the top of my head and encompassing my complete head. A voice says to me that he is Saint Francis of Assisi, and that he is the healer of Tami's healing group. He tells me that he is going to do psychic surgery on my heart to release my pain. I get a flash of a small knife and a poking sensation in my chest and then I feel the release of a waterfall of energy that is grounded by me into the center of the Earth. This lasts for nearly an hour while I sit with my eyes closed slowly feeling the pressure and tension dissipating from my being.

Over the next three to four days, I find myself experiencing a multitude of different symptoms – blurry weepy eyes, bags around my eyes, red and inflamed eyes that itch, a prickling sensation all over my body, and intense fatigue. The feeling of being ill is paramount. There are even instances where I feel that I am so sick that I might not make it. Over those three to four days, I slowly improve and find my symptoms disappearing. As I slowly recover from those symptoms, I get a couple of waves of repeating symptoms until the feeling of being ill dissipates.

In my mind, it is clear as day that what I experienced was nothing else other than a saving by Saint Francis, along with Tami's guide Joseph, who visited me later that night and told me that what had occurred with me was a very special event that I should journal about. I firmly and completely believe that each of us have guides watching out for us and protecting us on the other side. I feel grateful and blessed to have received this healing and blessing. Thank you!

Her experience was definitely extraordinary. Other people often report feeling an overall sense of peace, and on group healing days that things just feeling better and brighter. I recommend not comparing your experience to anyone else's, as all are different. I actually consider this book a form of group healing because I have been intentional to infuse loving energy into each word you read.

Your Divine Essence

Inner-work isn't fun, but it is one of the most rewarding things you will do in your life. It's the ultimate way to transform yourself. I hardly resemble that girl I was in high school. Her experiences and lessons exist within me, but the way I respond and love life is much different. Yet, without my journey through suicide, bullying in college (forgot to mention that one), autism, Lyme disease, and intense grief, I may not have been able to uncover who I am and shine that into the world.

We all have one thing in common that cannot be denied. We were all created with a spark of God within us. We all hold that light. I have seen it in my dreams and my visions. I have seen it within ones that would be considered riddled in darkness. There is still a light there. It may be very dim and hard to see, but it is there. Our journey is about healing that which hinders our light from illuminating and shining God's pure love into the world.

When you connect with that light within you, you connect with the Source energy of pure unconditional love. The more you connect to that light, the more it expands. As you make the commitment in your life to expand your light into the world, the things which hinder you are revealed. It may seem like you are on a roller coaster as issues rise to the surface, yet they are revealed to release and be healed. With every layer comes new understanding and your divine essence shining and illuminating more love into the world. The whole being evolves from stuckness to freedom and vibrancy.

All that you have done in your life leads you to this moment. The choice is presented to you. Do you want to live your soul purpose? Do you want to release yourself from the old ways that have hindered you? Are you ready to shine love in all things you do? In that choice is where your relationship with your child stands in question. A new way awaits you, a way where you can make choices intuitively and with love and acceptance, without an agenda tainting the joy.

As you uncover your divine essence, you are going to find something out. Maybe I shouldn't spoil the surprise by telling you. If I told you, you may not believe me. Ok, here goes.....YOU ARE AWESOME! You have the power to create, to love, to be happier than ever before. Your thoughts turn to reality. The more you clear out the crud, the more the love and divine power shines through. Absolute miracles can become everyday occurrences that you are blessed to bear witness. Epiphanies become the mainstay and with each one, we become more humble and more grateful for the experiences. By purchasing this book and reading this far, you have opened yourself to that opportunity. I am blessed and grateful to be a small part in your journey, planting seeds of knowledge from my experiences, which you can now choose to allow those seeds to take root or not. It's all up to you. You can be and are an instrument of peace.

Daily Practice and Self-Care

As a mom that learned the hard way, part of my journey is to help parents to understand how they just cannot take the back seat when it comes to self-care. All of the techniques we discussed in this book are for your child but also every single member of your family, including yourself. As a parent, we may have difficulty in spending that time on ourselves as we try to take on everything ourselves. A shift in priorities may be in order here and not allowing the emotion of guilt to infest your mind, because you are just as deserving and worthy of health and happiness as your child. It can be done where all receive what they need, including you.

Here are some examples of how you can integrate vibrational healing into your daily life for yourself and the entire family:

1. Carve out at least 20 minutes twice per day to bring in the light and peace. It doesn't exist outside of you, it is more of an awakening to the light and peace within you. This is accomplished during undistracted, dedicated time to this purpose. Meditation, yoga, chanting, quiet time, soft music and other ways can be used. The key here is absolutely no technology should be in your presence as it is our greatest distraction. Help your husband find the time to do this too and he can help you find the time. During this time you should be open to receiving and allowing guidance, but not controlling or demanding of it.

2. All food, supplements and drink should be infused with loving energy. Hold your hands over the items and ask blessings that it be infused with love. Imagine each bite or each drink bringing divine energy into each and every cell of your body. (And that of your family.)

3. Be aware of your thoughts and how they affect your day. Notice any outside influences such as friends, acquaintances or social media in which there is a lot of negativity. Consider taking a break from those influences. Pay attention to any new influences and if you are triggered towards toxic emotional responses. Even a break from watching the news or certain TV shows can shift your energy in a positive way.

4. Notice the energy around you from others and what you are putting into the world. Can you be infusing more love and compassion into your communications? Old toxic communication patterns can be adjusted by running it through the vibration of love. If it isn't loving and compassionate, don't say it or type it. We can't force others to change their energetic imprint but you are responsible for yours. Know this and understand it.

5. Pay attention to the signals in your physical body. Do you feel tense or relaxed? Stay open to allowing your body to speak to you and tell you what it needs. Connect with your body and ask for its messages. It has a voice of its own and you can receive those messages easily.

6. Spend some time in nature each day, even if it is with your kids at the park. As they play, feel the energy of the trees, the Earth, and notice the birds and animals around you. Connect in some way. Connect with the Earth at this time to help bring the grounding energy into your body.

7. Do at least one thing each day that brings you joy. For me, it usually comes through music or dancing. I found a beautiful practice called *Chakradance* and have had some amazing experiences with it. After a *Chakradance* session, I feel fully grounded, completely balanced at all levels, alive, awakened and at peace. You may find your joy through singing, dancing, walking, crafting, taking pictures, scrapbooking or calling your best friend. Just pick something each day and do it.

8. Lastly, always put gratitude out into the Universe. What are you grateful for? As I am drifting off to sleep at night, I often will choose one person and think about all I am grateful for with this person. It's often someone I struggle with and I decide to see the light within them and send my gratitude to that part of them. It's amazing how you can forget about all the annoying experiences with them when you focus on them only through gratitude. I find that by sending this out there, I also feel peace and relaxation through my own body. Just as Michael showed me....as I send healing to others, it heals myself. (Yet, that is the side benefit, the true intention is just to send it out there with no expectations.)

Remember, when struggles come up, and they always do, ask the question: What am I supposed to learn here? You will know. You will grow. You will show your divine essence in all that you do.

Chapter 14:
Deepening Your Connections

My vision for you is so clear now. I feel you already deepening your connections with yourself and your family. I see you looking back from the future today and saying, "How can my life be so amazing?" There is so much beauty in store for you, and the love I feel for your journey is bursting from my heart to yours.

Your path is becoming so clear now and your heart is understanding and resonating with the words. You are alive and the possibilities are endless. Can you join me in this vision of your life? In your life you…

- Are aligned with your soul purpose.

- Understand the soul purpose of those around you and support them.

- Understand how other's journeys are different from your own, and shouldn't be judged, but allow space for their growth in their timeframe.

- Are deeply connected to others at the heart level. With your loved ones, the flow of love is constant and steady. The love is unconditional and can never be harmed or broken, it is flowing and constant.

- Love all parts of your child, even parts that may seem ill or diseased. You love those parts for showing you the lessons they bring. You accept those parts as teachers and give gratitude for the lessons.

- Understand the intentions behind some behaviors. You aren't embarrassed. You know that others have much to learn about their own flexibility, hidden emotions and issues in which your child may stimulate in them with his behavior. You understand that his behavior may bring hidden gifts to yourself and others.

- Are aware of what hinders you and are constantly trimming and pruning the weeds of your past to allow for new growth in your now moment.

- Are responsible for your responses, actions, compromises, allowances and intentions and own up to that.

- Are in the flow and able to create and manifest amazing things in your life.

- Are modeling a beautiful example for your children and others to live their truth and live in their divine power. You hold space for them until they can live it themselves.

- Are vibrating at a higher level, which naturally reflects the love energy in you out to others where they can discover their own light.

- Understand that your emotions are real and honored as part of the human experience and expressed naturally where they flow freely and beautifully.

- Know that your mind and ego are not the enemy, but parts of you that make you the beautiful you that you are. You are aware when one becomes dominant over your light and gently bring them back to balance along with all parts of you.

- Know that your Spirit and Soul are constant, never dying and always bringing you lessons to awaken you to new knowledge. They are the true essence of who you are and are perfect in every way. Our journey here is to remember that. We forgot once, and now we know.

This last point reminds me of one of my very favorite hymns, *Amazing Grace*.

"….I once was lost, but now I'm found, was blind but now I see."

I want to thank you for giving me the opportunity to share my experiences with you. My faith is that you will now be more open to understanding your child and yourself more deeply and use vibrational healing as a wonderful method to bring balance and peace into your world.

Blessings and love from my house to yours,
Tami

Resources

This is a list of my favorite resources for Vibrational Healing and also some things mentioned in the book you may want to know about.

Tami Duncan's website:
http://www.EpiphanyHealingArts.com

World Autism Meditation:
http://www.spreaker.com/user/epiphanyhealingarts

Epiphany Healing Arts Facebook Page:
https://www.facebook.com/pages/Epiphany-Healing-Arts/143010365788483

Family Awakenings for Awesome Kids: Online class
http://www.epiphanyhealingarts.com/Family_Awakenings_Course.html

Group Healing Program:
http://www.epiphanyhealingarts.com/Group_Healing.html

Chakradance: I recommend either finding a class in your area or purchasing the 7 Keys to Freedom DVD or Dawn to Dusk CD. You can enter in "Tami" as a coupon code and get a small discount. www.chakradance.com

Essential Oils:

It is important to order from a company that has quality oils. There are three companies that I recommend. I also believe it is important to work with a knowledgeable representative that understands each oil and their unique properties and knows how to use them safely. I don't want to send you to just "anyone" because I want your person to be educated. Therefore I am only listing one person from each company.

DoTERRA:
http://www.mydoterra.com/remedyblends/

Young Living:
http://www.myautismhatrack.com/essential-oils.html

Floracopeia:
www.floracopeia.com David Crow has many educational opportunities and certifications on his website.

Flower Essences:

Bach Flower Remedies can be found at your local health food store.

Bach Flower Remedies for Children: A Parent's Guide – by Barbara Mazzarella

Australian Bush Flower Remedies:
http://ausflowers.com.au

One Willow Apothecary:
http://www.onewillowapothecaries.com

Alaskan Essences:
http://www.alaskanessences.com/products/
They also carry Gem Elixirs which are made from the essence of crystals and can be very powerful vibrations as well. Purification is the blend that can be used to clear negative energy from the space.

Flor-Alchemy:
http://www.floracopeia.com/Store/Flower-Essence-Products/
This company also has educational classes on how to use the flower essences.

Muscle Testing:

Muscle Testing Made Easy Online Class:
http://www.epiphanyhealingarts.com/Muscle_Testing_Made_Easy.html

Arm Length Test by Uwe Albrecht, MD
https://www.youtube.com/watch?v=C7EPVzGZhBE

Autonomic Response Testing by Dietrich Klinghardt (practitioner courses):
http://www.klinghardtacademy.com/Articles/ART-Laws.html

Core Belief Work:

http://www.highvibrations.net/private_practitioners.html #side_priv_pract

Practitioner Training Program
I am in the process of creating a certified practitioner training program using a unique form of energy healing in client sessions. Please check the website for the class schedule: www.EpiphanyHealingArts.com

Home Healers Training
This is a special workshop training for parent to learn vibrational healing techniques they can easily implement at home without a practitioner.
www.EpiphanyHealingArts.com

Energy Healing Recommendations
Nathalie La Forest – www.nathalielaforest.com
Kim Quinn – www.conceptsinclarity.com
Angie Mercier – www.angeliquemercier.wix.com

Other Stuff:

Thinking Mom's Revolution:
www.ThinkingMomsRevolution.com

Intuitive Homeopathy: www.IntuitiveHomeopathy.com

Book Recommendations:

The Other Side of Autism by Laura Hirsch

Waiting For Weston by Marilu Schmier

AWEtizm by Lyrica Mia and Gayle Barkley Lee

About the Author

Tami Duncan is a mom of two kids, one who was diagnosed with autism and Lyme disease. When she found out that she and her son both had Lyme disease, she started a non-profit foundation which provides support and education for families and physicians. She also co-authored a book called *The Lyme-Autism Connection"* with Bryan Rosner.

During her twelve-year journey through autism, biomedical interventions, therapies and Lyme disease she awakened to her own spiritual gifts, realizing that when she integrated energy healing and spiritual practices into her treatment for herself and her son, big things happened. She dove in headfirst and became a student of the Universe and trained in Reiki, Vibrational Healing, Shamanic Techniques, Multi-Dimensional Frequencies, Garcia Innergetics, Mediumship, Channeling, Essential Oils, Flower Essences, Telepathic Communication, Innerwise, Holographic Healing, and many more techniques given to her through spiritual guidance. She considers herself both a student and a teacher.

Tami has a thriving business called Epiphany Healing Arts, in which she helps families with children diagnosed with autism in numerous ways. She offers various online classes and workshops, in addition to doing private phone sessions with parents to get messages from their child that she receives telepathically. She has a special place in her heart for families affected by autism and chronic illness.

11510678R00123

Printed in Great Britain
by Amazon.co.uk, Ltd.,
Marston Gate.